From The Book:

Lawyers can bump jurors from the panel with no duty to explain why, even if the reasons are prejudicial. Forget the idea of a "fair and impartial" jury. If you're an executive, don't expect a "jury of your peers." The majority of jurors might be housewives, factory workers, and the unemployed.

Most litigation sucks resources from the world. Lawsuits usually do nothing but make people miserable. The process haunts plaintiffs and defendants alike. It drives at their sanity and makes them all less productive.

Judges are predisposed in many areas and they need to face it. They're prejudiced against blacks, whites, women, men, gays, dogs, owls, and Catholics. They're human; experiences shaped their beliefs. But, judges do a most respectable public service: wash the country's dirty laundry.

Our judicial system never exonerates a defendant. The names of William Kennedy Smith, Woody Allen, and even Clarence Thomas (in Senate hearings) forever carry the stigma of the charges, and the shadow of suspicion.

In our appellate courts, something is terribly amiss when more consideration is given as to whether a trial was procedurally fair than if the accused was really guilty.

Any attorney who contributes to a judge's campaign for re-election or endorses a candidate should be barred from practicing before that judge. No case should be decided because of a generous contribution, and even the appearance of pandering influence should be banned.

Author Profile

Steve Bertsch is a 43-year-old Seattle attorney who specializes in representing the abused. Several of his noted cases involved Northwest Coast Indians.

He is an expert in cases of spouse and child abuse, defender of the mentally ill and the indigent, and a strong believer in animal rights.

A graduate of the University of Washington and Gonzaga University, Mr. Bertsch became a member of the Washington State Bar Association in 1978.

With his wife, Sue, the Bertsches have been actively involved in foster care and in specialized parenting programs.

They have a son, Devon, and a daughter, Stacy, not to mention two ponies, three cats, and two German shepherds.

In his spare time, Mr. Bertsch is a voracious reader, an inventor of games, and a frustrated marathon runner.

CRISIS
— IN OUR —
COURTS

[signature: Steve Bertsch]

by Steve Bertsch

illustrations by Mark Lewis

GOLLEHON BOOKS
GRAND RAPIDS, MICHIGAN

Library of Congress Catalog Card Number 93-79334

ISBN 0-914839-30-6
(International Standard Book Number)

GOLLEHON BOOKS are published by: Gollehon Press, Inc.,
6157 28th St. SE, Grand Rapids, MI 49546. GOLLEHON BOOKS are
available in quantity purchases; contact Special Sales. Gollehon does not
accept unsolicited manuscripts. Brief book proposals are reviewed.

Underlying Illustrations on pages x, xi, xii, and 64 Copyright ©1993
by Mark Lewis.

Don't look for premiums, coupons, or legal advice in this book. It won't help you divorce your spouse, parents, or anyone else. Nor is it intended to assist you in solving other personal legal matters. The book is a critical analysis of our legal system. Its design is to offer suggestions to correct numerous system flaws on a macro level, and its commentary should not be applied to individual cases.

Contents

Your Judge

Your Lawyer

Their Lawyer

Acknowledgments

The writing of this book would not have been possible without the wonderful support of many understanding people. They include, but in no way are limited to, the following:

My son Devon for tolerating endless questioning from me and assisting in research. My daughter Stacy for listening patiently and comforting me throughout the writing. And both of them for keeping the volume of their music below "booming" while I wrote.

All my friends, family members, and co-workers whose comments and assistance were greatly appreciated.

The staffs at the Snohomish County Law Library, the Lake Stevens Public Library, and the Everett Community College, without whose assistance this book would have been a much greater task.

Stanley and Sharon Bertsch, Elaine Gillett, Sandra Hasegawa, Martin Itter, William Rapp, John Rodgers, and James Young, who were patient enough to read the first draft of this book.

I am also grateful that many attorneys gave so freely of their time to discuss issues with me.

Special gratitude is extended to Judge Glenn Allen, Jr., former jurist of the Michigan Court of Appeals, who reviewed my manuscript and offered great insight.

And a final thanks to my publisher, John Gollehon, for his competent editing, thoughtful input, extreme patience, and for introducing me to Skeezer.

Steve Bertsch

To Sue

Preface

Crisis In Our Courts is tough on lawyers. Many fellow attorneys have expressed concern with it; some have asked me to soft-pedal. Others attempted to sour my publisher on the manuscript. But it's necessary to tell it as it is.

Crisis In Our Courts is a hard-hitting book than lays bare several defects in our legal system. That's not a reason to shelve it. Its message must be sounded. People need to take back the courts. A judicial system should serve, not enslave.

As with any writing that contains editorial, biases surface. In preparing this book, I attempted to analyze both sides, but my roots often found their way into the manuscript. I am a criminal defense attorney who occasionally opens a file containing a business matter. Any civil work I do is usually for the defendant. That means I generally represent people who have been sued (the sue-ees) or have been charged with a crime. I rarely counsel plaintiffs (the sue-ers) and am philosophically opposed to most plaintiff's cases. I don't have any use for get-rich-quick schemes. When I type a "p" for plaintiff, I hit the letter with as much cynicism as my little finger can swat at the keyboard. Further, I prefer representing little guys who face potential ruin from plaintiff's complaints if I don't perform well. The pressure is exciting.

Occasionally, the term "lawyer" is used loosely. In many instances when the word appears—or any synonym for it (attorney, barrister, counselor, solicitor, weasel, or schmuck)— it means *all* lawyers. In other instances, it refers only to a minority of the profession who do their best to convince the world that all lawyers are thieving swine. Regarding *voir dire* and *peremptory challenges,* all attorneys are guilty. However, when slimy tactics are mentioned, it generally applies to a select few. These Machiavellian Princes can be found in any profession, but they gather aplenty in the legal field, as they ferret out their living at everyone's expense.

If you were to split a dozen donuts with most attorneys, you would end up with at *least* six. Most lawyers I know are honest, ethical, and worthy of trust. This even includes the ones that begin with "p"s, the prosecutors and plaintiff's counsel. Many would gladly repair our system and make it more equitable, if they could. Read *Crisis In Our Courts* and you will discover why they can't escape from their microscopic loop long enough to perform a macro-level fix, no matter how well-intended they are. From the ethical lawyers, you would get no fewer than a half-dozen donuts.

However, a tiny percentage of "princes" would leave you with nothing but the holes. These "holy" advocates know who they are, and I offer no apologies for any offenses tendered them.

SB

CHAPTER 1

Courthouse Crap Shoot

Some games are based upon skill, such as chess. Others, like bingo, are settled by pure chance. Still others need both luck and skill, as in poker. Today, going to court is a game, too. There's a winner; there's a loser; and like poker, the outcome is decided by mixing luck and skill. Only the stakes are much higher. You could lose your freedom, or you could lose everything you own.

When a lawyer's skill totally outclasses the opposition, the verdict is usually automatic. The prosecuting attorney for Florida, Moira Lasch, discovered this when she met the country's elite while trying to convict William Kennedy Smith of rape. It didn't matter whether Smith was guilty or not; his cadre of attorneys would have crushed most prosecutors.

In most courtroom battles, the advocates are more evenly balanced, and then luck enters the case. Even the crafty, brilliant, and inventive lawyers often need it, or they lose. The brightest criminal lawyers frequently rely on Lady Luck to give them a panel full of stupid jurors who are gullible enough to believe the absurd. Crafty civil attorneys regularly pray for a jury packed with emotional twits who leave their common sense at home.

1

Overpowering lawyers and Lady Luck have turned our legal system inside out, leaving us with an inequitable mass of decisions. People shoot craps in our courtrooms every day—but our system is supposed to be better than that. Too often, justice loses to the rich, the powerful, and the lucky.

Judicial Crisis

The rules of the game are called *procedure,* which are baffling to most outsiders. Attorneys have mastered the procedural game, stacking the deck in their favor.

Our courts are in crisis. Overwhelmed by too many players, court calenders are so full that it takes months, sometimes even years, to get a case before a judge. When the impatient parties finally get their chance in the courtroom, they discover that justice takes a back seat to formal kowtowing. All too frequently, procedure dominates over substance. In court, the rules of procedure control nearly everything. Valid claims are dismissed for simple procedural mistakes while hair-brained suits flood the system because they meticulously follow the court's procedural maze.

Everyone has access to the courts, but only those with attorneys can effectively use the system. Any person foolish enough to represent himself quickly discovers the wrath of the rules. It matters not whether the case has merit, only that kowtowing is done properly. To assure a claim is heard, it's almost imperative to hire a lawyer to wind a case through a morass of rules and timetables.

Our courts are in crisis. Everyone knows it—everyone understands it—everyone has a solution. In restaurants, stores, laundromats, and on the street, people berate the ruined system. Each critic has an opinion or two about the crisis, and how to correct it. But nothing is done.

Criminal Chaos

When all the conflicting ideas for correcting the system are combined, it leaves total chaos. In the criminal arena two main factions do battle. One group uses a club to bludgeon our courts and cries, "Judges are too soft—be tougher on crime. Take all the criminals and shoot 'em. Or at least lock 'em up and lose the keys."

Another team shrieks that cops are brutal, jails are inhumane, and criminals are the true victims of our system. They seek rehabilitation of convicts, not punishment. Both groups think they're right, but we all know it can't be that simple.

Americans have a strong sense of justice—tempered with a like desire for retribution. The rule is that when someone breaks the law, they forfeit their freedom. For two decades, the law-and-order team has reigned supreme, imprisoning all the crooks at phenomenally increasing rates. With the attitude of "jail 'em all" we've developed a fetish for incarcerating people. On a per capita basis, we imprison four times as many people as our neighbors to the north. Our ratio is no better when compared to China. Prisons bulge beyond capacity despite the supposedly soft judges.

In 1992, 800,000 of our residents wore horizontal stripes on their sleeves and numbers on their chests. Our state prisons operate at between 15 and 31 percent *over* capacity. We've jailed so many people, we can't house any more. Judges might be responsible for some problems, but too soft on crime, they're not. Every time they sentence someone to jail, something has to give. Either space must be built for the new convict or another inmate must be released.

The Washington State prisons chief claims we're headed for disaster if we continue locking people up at today's pace. He said that if things continue at the current rate, by the year

2056 everyone in the state will be incarcerated or working for a corrections facility.

Lobbyist groups like Mothers Against Drunk Drivers have been effective in getting intoxicated yo-yos off the road, reducing traffic deaths. But decreasing our traffic fatalities has been a mixed blessing: Society will pay. Although streets are safer in one regard, they are deadlier in another. Many violent criminals get shorter sentences because beds in the jails are going to drunks. Indeed, intoxicated drivers are dangerous, and often deadly, but how are they any more a burden on society than the violent stalkers who prey on everyone? Why not let the drunks and the mashers sleep in the same bed? Isn't it ridiculous to have to choose?

We've waged a war on other drugs too, and incarcerated a huge number of people involved with dope. In the 1970s, about 10 percent of people jailed by states had committed drug offenses. Today, it's almost 30 percent. Before declaring war on mind-altering drugs, 60 percent of our lockups were for murder, manslaughter, assault, robbery, and burglary. Today, less than 40 percent fit into that category to make room for drug sellers and users.

"So what!" shout the law-and-order buffs. If we used the death penalty we'd have room for all the other crooks. Their logic is false. Were we to open season on all the country's killers awaiting the gas house or the electric chair, we'd create room for only another 2,600 inmates. Shooting the lot wouldn't solve the problem—2,600 beds won't touch the dilemma.

On the other side of the argument sit the heart-bleeding liberals. They advocate turning the motley crew of prisoners loose, but not before giving them proper education on how to live in the outside world without raping their neighbors. Rehabilitation is expensive and doesn't remove the core problem. Many prisoners are sociopaths; they don't want reform, and will menace whoever is near them. Some people must be locked in cells, permanently.

Whichever view you consider, our criminal justice system is laboring. Murderers go free on technicalities while innocent parties get convicted. Prisoners tie up our court system with endless appeals, and now they play another game. The inmates now sue society for civil wrongs. These suits aren't to make life less brutal in prisons. No, there's a higher purpose—to get rich. Our broken criminal system is bleeding its poison into non-criminal matters.

Civil War

Crossing over to the civil side of the law, citizens also have their opinions. Civil law is anything that isn't criminal. It's the system we use to settle disputes. When negotiation breaks down, and mediation fails, Americans seek civil remedies in court.

Most people think of civil law as litigation and legal suits. The complexities of the system baffle even the brightest lay people. The average person views the legal system as an unfathomable, untouchable, morass of legal gobbledygook. While headlines blaze out notices of huge jury awards for various injuries, most readers don't know whether the verdicts are fair and proper because they have no interest in untangling all the legalese to find out. And you certainly can't rely on newspaper accounts; they leave a lot to be desired.

A judge I've known for several years told me, "Steve, after listening to a case from the bench, I'm frightened of what might appear in the paper. Yesterday, I read a newspaper account of a court case. It was only after reading the reporter's byline that I realized it was *my* case. The report was so screwed up that I didn't even suspect it happened in my courtroom."

He said, "You know what, lawyers ought to write these." I told him the cost would be too high. He said, "Almost everyone relies on the media to tell them what happens in court—only attorneys can do it justice."

The fact is, if you don't sit in the courtroom and listen to the entire case, you're stuck with the media version. You don't know whether the report is accurate or if it is a twisted and sensationalized story. Worse than that, we receive only what the editor wants us to read; we let the media sort it out for us.

A case in point happened in Los Angeles. Almost everyone knows of the 80-second beating that Rodney King endured from the LAPD. But the case was far more complex than that, or else the trial would have been less than two minutes long. Many television broadcasts repeatedly showed the beating, but often neglected to show the portion where King charged at one of the officers—punching, kicking, and throwing a police officer from his back. Often ignored in the newscasts were these facts: King was double-drunk with a blood-alcohol level of nearly twice the legal limit. He had been paroled only two months before the beating. He was attempting to elude police pursuit at speeds up to 100 miles per hour. He presented a menacing appearance by his hulking size and hostile nature.

Expert Advice

Lay people competently form opinions about the criminal system by coupling pure emotion with common experience. People want to feel safe in their neighborhood. They don't want gangs running wild, or mashers stalking the alleys. It's easy to get mad at killers and scream for blood, but to make important decisions about civil cases, the average person can easily become confused.

Whether antitrust suits and other complex cases are right or wrong often get left to people who specialize in these highly esoteric matters. Intelligent people look to the experts for advice before forming opinions.

Unfortunately, once experts get into the picture, common sense often takes a detour. Wise people seek knowledge from those who should understand best. In so doing, the wise often disregard what they already knew and become the fools.

When a lawyer, doctor, priest, or scientist gives an opinion, people often hush, and listen intently. It's like those commercials about the broker whose advice quiets the crowd. The stockbroker's opinion need not be right, nor even reasonable to be considered. Sometimes the expert's position is accepted despite the knot it forms in the gut of the listener. Since the person talking knows the subject, their statements have instant credibility.

Once people discard their common sense and experience, they're ripe for brainwashing. Lawyers gladly handle this duty, instructing the legal ignoramuses about what's best for our country while protecting our rights. Talent-rich teams, led by the Ralph Naders, plaintiffs' lawyers, ACLU, and other consumer advocates appear to promote the litigation explosion. The import of their message is: Shocking judgments make people cautious, and the world's a safer place because of it. It's your duty to sue those dirty buggers.

To counter the argument in favor of lawsuit mania are some powerhouses led by religious groups, business organizations, insurance companies, the defense bar, and Dan Quayle. This group drivels on relentlessly that the lawsuit is the ruin of humanity. They claim that suing is counter-productive, and if we don't end our infatuation with litigation, America will lose its competitive edge.

Like the extremes on both sides of the criminal argument, the civil war can't be solved by either measure, no matter how well the experts think they understand the problem. There must be a middle ground, a place of reason. If the suit-happy experts convince us to sue harder, faster, and longer, society will lose productivity, jobs, and economic strength. If we follow the other side and severely limit lawsuits, every decent person would get trampled by greedy thugs and weasels.

But, there's still another deep-rooted problem with our courts. One that it seems everyone on the street knows, feels, and advocates. Lawyers are to blame, they say. They defend weasels and crooks who don't deserve any help. Lies are their best swords as they dig into honest people with outright trash. They assure their positions by writing incomprehensible legal babble into our laws so only experts—lawyers—can grasp it.

Attorneys have another game, one they play very well. It's litigation bingo. When an impoverished plaintiff with a terrible injury walks into a lawyer's office, the victim quickly gets interviewed. If it turns out that someone with money caused the injury, this pathetic person fills the lawyer's card. Bingo! Should the same individual come into the office under identical circumstances, except, a beggar caused the injury, things change. Since there's no chance of recovery, the poor victim is tossed out the door, discarded like moldy bread.

When lawyers think they have a case worth a few bucks, they clamp down on all parties who could be remotely responsible. To squeeze money from defendants, they tighten a legal vice by threatening to sue everyone in sight. The more lines in the water, the better the chance of catching a big fish.

Lawyers further terrorize the nation with persuasion tactics that if used outside their profession would go by another name—*blackmail*. They've set up the game so what's illegal for anyone else in the country to do is competent, aggressive, legal representation. They've cornered the market on sleaze.

It starts something like this: A lawyer contacts the maker of the drug that blinded his client and says, "Did you know that another manufacturer got hit for $125 million for a similar injury?" Another approach might be to say: "I'm gonna own your factory unless you settle this case!" Some attorneys use clubs and others use honey, but the result is the same.

Flaws and Fortune

In our suit-filled world we have some weird happenings. It used to be that when disaster struck a family, or even a region, the unfortunate victims sucked in their guts and struggled to start over. If a tornado swept through a town, or an earthquake cracked the earth, people got together and rebuilt. There would be government handouts for relief, and charity would flow from around the nation. After the devastation, it was hoped that the people would be able to come back from the brink of ruin.

You still see this charity at work today. When Hurricane Andrew hit Dade County, Florida, President Bush flew down and sent relief to the area. Presidential hopeful Bill Clinton did the same. Whether it was for political reasons or not, Florida received a great deal of aid. Tent cities were constructed for those whose homes were destroyed by the storm. The state pulled itself up from the tragedy, but it's scarred deeply.

In the wake of the infamous hurricane, *Knight-Ridder* published an account of how unethical people cashed in. The story is loaded with accounts of people who defrauded their insurance companies by claiming storm damage that never happened. One case involved a man who tore shingles off his roof so insurance would pay him for a new one. He felt no remorse because when he had an automobile accident, the insurance company paid out a $600 claim, but raised his rates by $300 a year. That sums up the attitude quite nicely: "Since insurers are the bad guys, let's steal from them."

The thieving effort was so widespread that a psychologist was interviewed who said the bilking was exacerbated by failed morals of the masses. The public gets encouragement since it's perceived that everyone's doing it. "It's a group contagion because there's group support." A minister said, "There is a morality surrounding disaster." There sure is—to cheat. It's the American way to get something for being knocked down—we learned it from our lawyers.

The same type of thing occurs when a single person gets slammed by catastrophe. They get help from their neighbors, aid from the state, assistance from the Red Cross, and try to start anew. There are some rare cases that the media draws attention to and broadcasts the plight of an individual's tragedy. To these, the public responds with donations far exceeding the loss. In these unusual circumstances, the victim profits from the tragedy.

Usually, when disaster strikes, people are made nearly whole by charity. Our civil system of justice has some of these same characteristics. When a party is injured by another, the law says the guilty one must make the other whole by putting the victim back into the same position as he was in before the accident.

The theory of making the wrongdoer pay is logical, noble, and just. Reason and common sense, items that often get lost in the legal jungle, shout for this type of equity. Judges attempt to slide the blame onto the responsible person who must pay the victim.

In theory, if Joe Innocent gets hit by Jane Reckless who ran a red light, Joe recovers from her for lost wages, medical expenses, and restoration of his car. Those are *special damages*. They're the real financial injuries. But civil law isn't happy to settle up with out-of-pocket costs, it adds in a kicker— general damages. *General damages* are the intangibles—injuries to the psyche and the soul. Lawyers call them pain and suffering, mental anguish, lost relationships, and broken emotional links in one's life chain.

General damages are great because there's no way to control them. Who is to say how much a mother suffered because her son was hospitalized from a wreck? Who can put a value on how much it's worth to a wife whose husband became impotent by mental anguish suffered since a crash? General damages are the life-blood of plaintiffs' attorneys. They line lawyers' pockets with silver.

If there's no lawyer involved, insurance adjusters size up the victim and decide how little they can pay in general damages and still settle the claim. To arrive at a value for general damages, adjusters usually multiply the special damages by some number to cover the injured person's pain and inconvenience. The company then presents the person with a check to make them whole.

That's how many accident claims are settled. The money is paid by the insurance company of the person who ran the red light, unless, they didn't have insurance, or their coverage was too little to cover the damage from the accident. Then the injured person's insurance pays the difference, or the victim makes it up out of his own pocket. In either event, he's not made whole, but is worse off than before the accident. So, he sues for the difference.

Assuming the jughead who hit him is broke, winning a judgment is useless. As we discussed in the case of the poor beggar earlier in this chapter, a "good" attorney must look to other sources to collect money. Creative lawyers do this every day, looking for someone with money who can be linked to the accident. This remote party is sued to make Joe whole, and then some.

To identify these remote defendants, lawyers might look to the city for improper placement or poor maintenance of the traffic light. The attorneys would chirp that this error made the intersection dangerous because the jughead couldn't see the signal was red. They might also look to the makers of Joe's and the jughead's cars for manufacturing defects. The good Samaritan who stopped to give aid becomes another target. Likewise, the police and the ambulance drivers who appeared at the scene all get lined up, along with the doctor who treated Joe. Lawyers stretch to find someone with money who can be made responsible, even if it's the jughead's third-grade teacher, who should have reported the pupil's color-blindness ten years ago.

With all these people on line, the lawyer goes to work, not to make Joe whole, but to get him as wealthy as possible under the circumstances. That's because the attorney takes a percentage of the haul, so legal fees climb as the size of the award rises. Briefly, that's how the system is out to make Joe *over*-whole.

The craziest thing about our judicial maze is how unfairly these awards get distributed. Let's assume a bank president ran the red light and hit poor Joe. That's a gold mine for him and his lawyer. Let Harry Homeless, a down-and-outer from the Bronx, crash into Joe's car, he's lucky to get half his out-of-pocket costs reimbursed. If at the same intersection, instead of getting crashed by another car, lightning struck his car, he must appeal to The Almighty for compensation. I'm sure God has plenty of resources, but it's awfully tough to serve Him with a summons and complaint.

When tragedy strikes, our system demands that the correct messenger delivers it, or the victim is in real trouble. In an automobile accident, it's ideal to be struck by the richest person on the road. It helps if he also fights with police and snarls at the jury. That's the stuff magic awards are made from. It's every lawyer's dream.

If the defendant is rich, surly, and despised, and did something terrible, a plaintiff might even get *exemplary damages*.

(Exemplary damages are assessed against defendants for horrid behavior—sometimes called *punitive damages*.) While general damages are the lawyers' silver, punitive ones are pure gold.

On the other side, let a poor person strike Joe dead, and watch the lawyers scurry to avoid his case. That is, unless some otherwise innocent bystander is in the wrong place at the wrong time who happens to have money falling out of his *deep pockets*.

To make matters worse—as if they could be—lawyers actually advertise for these gems. When the big awards come tumbling in, the media often hypes them, and resentful people start thinking about how to get on the lunch wagon for themselves. They call attorneys, and we get deluged with nutty suits, and sometimes the verdicts are beyond comprehension.

The Outer Limits

People sue for all kinds of reasons, and the results are all kinds of wonderful. In reading these cases, consider not only the size of the verdicts, but the absurdity of some of them:

Remember *Dialing for Dollars*, a game show from the '60s? Well, a street person from New Jersey learned how refusing *Dial* earned *dollars* by spurning baths. The smellier he got, the filthier rich he became. When the unkempt man took to the library, the odor offended librarians and patrons, so he was ejected from the facility several times. Stinko took care of those displeased by his reeking presence. He sued for harassment and settled for a quarter-million dollars and change. Perhaps Avon could capture his essence and market a new line, *The Million-Dollar Dream*.

A person who was misdiagnosed as suffering from AIDS filed a multi-million-dollar suit because of the error. A prison nurse who got AIDS from struggling with an inmate was awarded $5.3 million because the guards didn't help her. Another woman was awarded $6.6 million for receiving tainted blood that infected her. If you get cancer from Mother Nature, you get nothing. With AIDS, you get money whether you have the disease or not.

AIDS crushed free speech on a school bus in Washington State. When a 14-year-old student boarded the bus after an extended absence, the concerned driver asked him, "Do you have something serious, like AIDS?" The boy's parents did what any good parents should, they sued for defamation of character because the remark caused students to scorn their son. But is it really worth a lawsuit? What about a simple apology? If NBC can apologize to GM, why not a bus driver to a kid?

Children on a Minnesota school bus are about to learn sexual enlightenment. A 7-year-old girl sued her classmates for using profanity and talking dirty to her. The claim sounds of sexual harassment. If lawyers want to keep their meal-wagon running, I guess they have to start 'em young.

A prosecuting attorney in Bellingham, Washington, shook up the courts by charging an 11-year-old boy with felonious farting. In preparing a complaint against the youngster for assault on another student, the prosecutor decided to add a count of levity. The document says that after pushing a school-mate and knocking the boy's books from his hands, the assail-ant then passed gas when the victim bent down to retrieve his belongings. The attorney who prepared the charge claimed it to be an in-house joke that accidentally got filed. Did the lawyer strike out, or just whiff one?

So the crass prosecutor doesn't feel alone, he has company. A hundred miles south, in Seattle, a person decided to represent himself when charged with burglary. The defendant claimed he had been shot in the left buttock by the owner of the burgled shop. To prove his point, the accused dropped his pants to his ankles. Since the fellow chose not to wear undergarments that day, the judge and jury got a perfect moon shot. That's what police call corroborating evidence.

A television show, Michigan Outdoors, was forced into bankruptcy because the moderator claimed that a deer-scent product that was advertised as containing deer urine actually contained cow urine. The bovine blunder cost the show big bucks in a defamation suit (pardon the pun). Because the production company couldn't afford the cost of the appeal bond, they had to go off the air. Justice in America is expensive. The wealthy can afford it, the poor can get it free, and the middle-class don't have the money to buy it. But, more importantly, who has the time to catch deer urine in a specimen jar anyhow?

From Arkansas comes a case where you can't tell who to root for in the courtroom. A convicted rapist was castrated while awaiting his criminal trial. After the operation, the sheriff of the county displayed the rapist's testicles in a jar. At the civil trial it was argued that the sadistic sheriff "was holding these up like they were a trophy." The jury awarded the rapist $150,000 for the humiliation he suffered. Who said crime doesn't pay—not the eunuch from Arkansas.

A Spokane Community College student failed a course and traveled to court. Robbery, cried the undergraduate, and he sued, claiming he deserved at least a "C" grade for the course. The jury disagreed and held the student to be a flunky. This is a total waste of judicial time. It was bad enough for such nonsense to appear in Superior Court, but it also traveled into the Court of Appeals.

In a Pittsburgh office supply store, a 17-year-old cat was boss. He had a bad day, claimed a customer, who sued because it "came from nowhere" and clawed the unsuspecting shopper, leaving a tiny scar on the back of her wrist. Friends of the cat and patrons of the business apparently wanted to clear the critter's name—they contributed $2,000 for a defense fund. The victim sought at least $3,000, but lost because she showed neither damages nor that the cat was vicious. While this case shows that justice can prevail, isn't it sad that someone needs $2,000 for legal fees to fight off a $3,000 claim? In too many cases, only the lawyers win.

Dogs wind up in court for things other than leash violations. Zsa Zsa Gabor was reportedly kicked off a Delta flight for letting her dogs loose on the plane. She sued the airlines for $10 million, alleging that she wasn't treated "in a first-class manner." It's not too surprising she released her pets on the airplane. The woman was once quoted in *Newsweek* as saying: "I love animals and children. People I could do without."

A New York couple bought a tombstone and paid for a grave site in a pet cemetery. Their dog was to have been buried with a pink blanket, toys, and a collar. Instead, the morticians tossed the dog into a mass grave. When the couple uncovered the fraud, they sued, and won an incredible judgment. The court awarded them $1.2 million. While the behavior of the defendants was deplorable, how could a case like this approach a million-dollar injury? Why should anyone play lotto with court cases like this waiting to be plucked?

The parents of a young girl might have been influenced by cases like the wrongly buried dog. Their daughter was killed and taken to a funeral home. The clothing worn by the girl was lost by the mortician, leaving her family in mourning. It seems that an ancient Native American burial rite is impossible to perform because the girl's clothing must be burned to speed the journey of the decedent into the hereafter. While it's sad that the rite of passage can't be performed for this Lakota girl, what good will a money judgment do? If we start getting into this type of suit, pretty soon we'll see the clergy brought to the courts for negligent baptismals and fraudulent conversions that kept a person from going to heaven.

In a different twist on the hereafter, a Tulsa widow sued a television evangelist for writing letters about his talks with God. According to the woman, the minister claimed that the woman's husband would be cured of illness, and promised a miracle because God wanted to restore her husband's health. The woman contended that the preacher wrote the letters after the man had died, and the widow had so informed the clergyman. The widow claims fraud and wants $40 million. Who is she going to put on the stand to prove the minister didn't talk to God? We're opening the courts to matters far beyond their competence.

Court time is often wasted on trivial matters, especially in divorce proceedings. A New York couple are fighting like kids and dogs. Their 2-year-old son received a puppy for Christmas from his father. Now that the divorce has heated up, dad tried to take the dog back. The court ruled that the boy and his dog must stay together. Judges need to throw this type of trash out of the courtroom. It belittles the proceedings and encourages people to fight over wooden nickels and zoo passes.

Juries are known for their largess. Headlines of excessive verdicts commonly cover the newspapers. People on the jury must figure, "So what if one person gets too much—it ain't coming from me." In Salt Lake City an elderly lady wanted a soft drink. She took a pair of pliers and tried opening a bottle of *7-Up* with them. The cap flew into her eye, so she sued the soda manufacturer. According to the judge, the jury was "inflamed with passion" when it awarded $10.5 million for the accident. The judge reduced the verdict to $375,000.

In a complex racketeering trial, reputed mobsters were acquitted on 77 counts after 22 months of trial. The reason— jurors misunderstood the court's instructions. The jury said the instructions confused them into wrongly thinking that if all twelve jurors didn't agree as to guilt, then the verdicts must all be not guilty. Justice was aborted because of legal babble and a stupid jury.

Wild Canadian geese frequented a pond on the property of a restaurant. One fateful day, a former chef of the restaurant stood near the pond and was allegedly attacked by an angry goose. While attempting to avoid jabs from the honker's beak, the cook fell backward over the root of a tree. The fall broke the chef's back, hospitalized him, and ruined his honeymoon. Like any good, former employee, he sued the restaurant for $1 million. Now, everyone's honked off.

The riots at Attica prison did more than kill a few people. Prisoners allegedly executed three inmates and a guard, while the police gunfire reportedly killed 29 inmates and ten hostages. With all that death, a lawsuit was certain. Former prisoners filed a $2.8 billion suit. The judge sat through the trial, but while the jury deliberated, he took a vacation to the Caribbean. When lawyers and jurors had questions, they gathered around a tiny speaker phone and listened as rulings squawked from the judge. Not only did the judge show disregard for the parties, jurors, and the lawyers, his behavior belittled the whole judicial process. The court case wasn't even important enough to delay a vacation. Talk about the long arm of the law, the only people who could enjoy this type of development own stock in AT&T.

When a mugger robbed a tourist in San Francisco, he began his trek down the easy path to money. A good-Samaritan cab driver who saw the theft got into the fray. He chased down the robber and pinned him against a building with his cab. The robber was busted in two ways—the cab broke his leg. Rather than sit quietly, the convict sought retribution, and committed judicial robbery. While serving a 10-year sentence for the theft, the mugger sued the cabby for using excessive force. Incredibly, the jury agreed with the mugger, and awarded him almost $25,000. With idiotic verdicts like this, it's no wonder that the cries of a woman being raped and killed in Central Park go unanswered.

Thankfully, the judge was a little brighter than the jury, and overturned their verdict. However, he didn't throw the case out, but ordered a new trial. Whoever said the only justice is for lawyers must have been thinking about a case like this.

A talk-show host at KGO radio in San Francisco started a fund to help the cabby to help pay the award. In less than a week, contributions exceeded the amount of the judgment. At least some people in the Bay Area understood that the cab driver needed relief from a system gone awry.

To get a further idea of where muggers' rights are headed, consider a New York thug. While he was robbing a senior citizen in a subway, police shot him. Wounds from the gunshot paralyzed him, so the robber sued and got an award of $4.3 million. If the crooks don't get your wallet on the streets, they get it in court. It seems like people who undertake violent criminal activity should assume the risk of any injuries they get, but not in New York or San Francisco. These two verdicts do nothing but ring a dinner bell for creeps to invade our courts.

Another New York convict, a killer, had an accident while serving his sentence. He lost a hand in a woodworking machine. The jury gave the poor devil $2.7 million. Why should criminals go to work when they can go to court?

Twisting the "devil made me do it" theme, a person serving a life sentence for homicide, sued Upjohn Co. for the side effects of the drug Halcion. This man claims no responsibility for killing another human. The drug made him do it. The prisoner wants $5.5 million. If this claim wins, can you imagine how many suits there'll be against *Anheuser-Busch* for making the poor drunks kill people with their cars? People must take responsibility for their own actions, but it will never happen if lawyers continue to take on cases like this one. Muggers and murderers shouldn't be given anything in civil court for the crimes they committed.

The *Chicago Tribune* reported that inmates in New York jails have put together a get-rich-quick scam. It is alleged that the scheme works like this: An inmate pays a guard or a lawyer to smuggle a gun into the facility. After getting the gun, the inmate either shoots himself, or directs someone else to do so. Then, the inmate sues the facility for not making it a safe place to do his time by allowing guns to be smuggled into the joint. At least five of these suits are pending, one seeking damages of $8.5 million.

A patient with testicular cancer had 39 vials of his sperm frozen and stored in a New Mexico sperm bank. The sperm thawed and died when the laboratory's cooling system failed. Armed with his wife and outrage, the man went to court and won $135,000. This is a classic case of putting all your sperm in one basket. Why didn't the man use two banks? In the computer age, everyone knows to make back-up copies of important matters.

The widow of a brewery employee claimed that because her husband took advantage of the free beer provided by the employer, he became an alcoholic and eventually was fired because of the debilitating disease. She won $85,000 in workers' compensation benefits. What's a drunk doing working in a brewery? Does this mean every fatty who works in a bakery can sue for being tempted by frosting?

As so often happens, a drunk driver took an innocent person's life. Since the drunk in this case was uninsured and broke, the victim's family looked elsewhere for money. They got a settlement from a retail store that sold the drunk a bottle of vodka that he drank elsewhere. In our battle to avenge deaths caused by drunk drivers, we've stretched the theory of liability beyond reason. If you can sue the store that sold a bottle, why not the landlord who leased the premises to the store. And why not the bank that carried the landlord's mortgage—and Boris Yeltsin for running the country that made the stupid vodka?

While in a bar in Saint Louis, an attorney allegedly grabbed a law student by her hips and bit her on the rump. After performing his feat, the lawyer reportedly laughed and exchanged high-fives with his friends. The woman bit back, winning a $27,500 verdict against him. In his defense, the assailant said he considered his action a compliment to the lady. I wonder what he'd do to insult her.

Some of these cases are samples of legal absurdity that choke our legal system. For every crazy case, a valid one had to step aside. Each nutty award had two sides—one side benefited from the judicial idiocy while the loser paid dearly for it. Our high-handed justice is dispensed unevenly and unfairly.

While our courts are in crisis, it's controllable. It can be corrected. The man on the street still holds the reigns, even if he doubts it. Our gluttonous judicial system can be organized, bumped, pushed, and prodded back into being a public servant, rather than a ruling tyrant.

CHAPTER 2

Jury Rigging

Fair Jury: (Common-Law Definition) *An impartial and indifferent group of competent people sworn to hear evidence and render a truthful verdict.*

Fair Jury: (Lawyer's Definition) *A group of people who vote for my client.*

A red-haired woman squirmed as she sat in the jury box. A trace of moisture dampened her upper lip. She remembered the judge telling her group to expect some tough personal questions. Since the lawyers were looking for "fair and impartial" persons to sit on the case, her background was important. The judge instructed her to be candid when answering the lawyer's questions. In a moment, she would enter the twilight zone.

"Mrs. Juryhopeful, what do you do for a living?" asked Joe Lawyer.

"I teach fifth grade."

Immediately, Joe Lawyer looked to the bench and said, "Your Honor, I would respectfully ask the court to excuse this juror."

Flustered, embarrassed, and understandably confused, the woman wandered out of the courtroom. Being stricken from the panel left her aghast. How could anyone judge her to be prejudiced after asking only one question?

What Mrs. Juryhopeful experienced was rejection by way of a *peremptory challenge*. It is an absolute right given attorneys in almost all courts in our country to discard a certain number of jurors from the panel without having to give a reason. The lawyer ripped her from the panel because he disliked something about her. It could have been her height, personal appearance, hair color, race, sex, or occupation. She never finds out why she was plucked from a jury because many reasons for the dismissal are illegal.

A federal law makes it illegal to exclude a citizen from a jury because of race, color, religion, sex, national origin, or economic status, but attorneys slyly circumvent this law with total impunity. The lawyer bumped Mrs. Juryhopeful and had no duty to explain his reason, even if the reason was illegal.

Every trial by jury has some form of this brutality. Most attorneys have the decency to ask a few questions and make it appear fair, but the result is the same. She's gone, probably because of her job. Attorneys want to educate the jury in the law and the facts of the case, but many fear that teachers will not oblige. The theory is that teachers know all of the answers and are not prone to listening to reason. As unfair as this stereotyping may seem, it happens every day under the guise of a search for a "fair and impartial" jury.

The only check on this enormous power of exercising a *peremptory challenge* comes from the lawyers themselves. Their integrity and morality are all that prevent abuse. Anyone who would let a fox count eggs at a chicken ranch would trust attorneys to be fair in their challenges.

Of course, some prospective jurors with an obvious bias have to be chucked from the jury. Indeed, lawyers have another tool for pruning what they perceive as bad wood from the tree of justice: It's called *challenge for cause*. An attorney can challenge the juror for being prejudiced against or partial to a litigant. A cause challenge would occur if the plaintiff were a teacher attempting to get pension benefits from a school district and the juror is on the school board. There is an obvious and immediate conflict of interest that would make that juror biased. A juror who is too prejudiced to listen to the case with an open mind should be dismissed for cause. Most authorities believe the reasoning for this type of removal is sound. If a party faced a jury composed of people with either hatred or love for that person, the verdict would be tainted by those emotions. The challenges for cause must remain if we are to have fair trials. We don't want a litigant's brother or neighbor on the jury.

Lawyers worry about the jurors for a significant reason. Herald Fahringer, a noted commentator on juries, wrote an article with the assertion that: "Jury selection is the most important part of any criminal trial... In most cases, the defendant's fate is fixed after jury selection." This is the opinion of a well-respected legal scholar. It's implications are tragic. It says that what happened is irrelevant—it only matters who will judge.

While there are those who would disagree with Fahringer, an honest poll of trial attorneys probably would concur. In my experience it is absolutely correct. I use the selection process in several ways, not the least of which is to make friends with as many jurors as possible. I find that the time spent building friendships on the panel wins cases for my clients.

Trial attorneys are placed in a terrible dilemma. If they want to win for their clients, they must use every legal tool available to them to build a favorable jury. These include peremptorily bumping offending panelists who would either make it more difficult to win or easier to lose.

Lawyers must zealously rig the jury with "winners." All lawyers have this duty, even for the most despicable mass-murderers. Attorneys are ethically bound to effectively advocate for their clients. If, as Fahringer suggests, jury selection is the most important part of a criminal trial, then the lawyers need to do their best work in that phase. Lawyers must ruthlessly build a biased jury. Until the rules are changed, these are the rules we play by.

To Serve or Not to Serve

Watch an entire trial and you must endure jury selection, something that the *Perry Mason* show always omitted. Hollywood ignores this process because it's too boring to interest anyone. But sometimes an actual trial—such as those of Mike Tyson and William Kennedy Smith—will get so much publicity that network television carries it live, complete with boring jury selection. The boredom is necessary because in our country a trial can't begin until the entire jury is selected by counsel and sworn in by the judge. In fictional portrayals of trials, the jury is just present. Filmmakers graciously overlook the selection process. In reality, of course, a painstaking screening occurs before the jury hears a case.

Jury members come from various lists compiled by the court administrator. The pool selected must form a cross-section of the community, and can't discriminate against any particular group. Courts have gone to great lengths to make these jury pools adequately represent the community.

Federal law dictates that a person is qualified to serve on a jury if the person is over 18 years old, a citizen of the country, and has resided at least one year in the district. Also, that person can be excluded if he or she can't read and write English well enough to fill out a juror qualification form, can't speak English, is physically or mentally incapacitated, or has been convicted of or awaiting trial on a felony.

Our courts go far beyond these statutory requirements in assessing juror qualifications. Their capability is determined by several other factors, ostensibly to help both parties find "fair and impartial" people for the jury. It sounds so righteous that everyone agrees that it is necessary to have an unbiased jury. The theory is that if people have made up their minds as to guilt or fault before listening to the case, they can't give a fair hearing of the evidence. An ideal jury has members who know nothing about the case before it begins, know none of the participants, and lack express or latent prejudices that will affect their judgment.

Additionally, the jury should ideally be composed of one's peers. After all, the phrase "jury of your peers" is basic to most people's understanding of what a jury is all about. But, once again, another flaw in the system rears its ugly head. If you're a business executive, forget the idea of having other business executives on your jury. If you're an actress, forget the notion of having thespians on your jury. If you're a crook, forget about having other crooks on your jury.

In truth, the ideal jury never sits on a case. If there has been any publicity, the jurors may know something about it. If it's a widely publicized case, they may know a great deal. Some may have decided who is wrong in the case. When there is massive publicity in a criminal trial, the defense attorney usually calls foul. The lawyer contends that it is impossible to get a fair trial because too many people have already decided the issue of guilt. The attorneys always demand fairness, but what they really want is victory.

When interviewed by *ABC's Nightline*, F. Lee Bailey claimed that in these cases the defense might be blowing smoke. He said that the more publicity a trial receives, the more likely a person is to be found "not guilty." The reasoning behind this is simple: Everyone dares the jury to be fair and impartial. The judge reminds them to be fair, then the prosecutor asserts the same desire. Defense counsel follows by claiming that impartiality is next to godliness. The jury logically draws the conclusion that they must be fair. But such daring attempts to convince the jury to be fair can actually make the jury vote not guilty for fear of showing a bias.

Bailey, who represented many celebrated defendants, including the Boston Strangler and Patty Hearst, stressed that the jury can't win. If they vote for conviction, they are accused of being unable to shake their belief of the defendant's guilt that the press put into their minds before the trial. They can only show fairness by acquitting the defendant. Bailey supports his position by saying that in the 20 most publicized cases he has seen, there were 16 not-guilty verdicts. That greatly exceeds the average acquittal rate.

If Bailey is correct, then the more the press reports on an upcoming trial, the better it is for the defendant. Ironically, a leading case on the subject of abusive pre-trial publicity resulted in a jury verdict of guilty. The accused hired an attorney, one F. Lee Bailey, to appeal the verdict. Bailey doggedly clamored error because the press had crucified an innocent man. Bailey won the appeal, and freedom for his client, Dr. Sam Sheppard.

There are times, though, when there is so much publicity, that attorneys want to take their show to another city (*change of venue*), hoping that the publicity is only focused locally. But what do you do when the publicity is national in scale?

When Melvin Belli represented Jack Ruby for the slaying of Lee Harvey Oswald, he was forced to try the case in Dallas. That community was shaken. The president had just been assassinated there and the prime suspect was murdered on national television. Dallas wanted to save face—it wanted vengeance. Belli called the Dallas area a "cesspool of prejudice." After his client was convicted, the outspoken attorney placed the blame on the jury: "I got a jury of bums."

Maybe, but for those of you old enough to remember, millions saw the accused on live national television. And they saw the "smoking gun." If that case would have been taken to the uppermost tip of Alaska, it wouldn't have made an icicle's worth of difference.

Prejudicial Pursuit

The American criminal justice system has a procedure built into it to offset the effects of pre-trial publicity. It is called *voir dire,* which is pronounced Vor DEAR, or Vwah DEAR, and simply means the process of quizzing jurors. Remember the case of our school teacher at the beginning of this chapter? That was voir dire in action. The sham search for truth commences by questioning a person by the judge or legal counsel. While either witnesses or jurors can be subjected to it, for now it will be treated solely for jury qualification.

Voir dire could just as well be articulated as voyeur (which rhymes with lawyer). During voir dire, jurors are quizzed by lawyers and judges for a single, noble purpose (if you believe the lawyers). That is, to expose a juror's bias for or against litigants. A skeptic might view the process as Brainwashing 101—or a lawyer's quest for fools.

In voir dire, the lawyers find out things about the jurors in various ways. They can see visually if a person is Hispanic or black, male or female, neat or sloppy. They can ask if a person is employed or unemployed, married or unmarried, faithful or unfaithful.

As seen in the William Kennedy Smith trial for rape, wealthy defendants can afford to hire body-language specialists to assess whether a juror is likely to favor the state or the defense. According to an interview on *Nightline*, these experts cost up to $500,000 for a single trial. Few people can afford this kind of luxury. I know of many rape defendants who hired attorneys to try the entire case for $5,000. That included investigation, lawyer time, and representation in court. Wealthy defendants have 100 times the poor man's total resources to spend on just the selection of jurors.

If the parties have enough resources, voyeuring begins long before voir dire occurs in the courtroom. Wealthy litigants subject jurors to covert pre voir dire. Detectives and other snoops drive by jurors' homes to see where they live and how their yards are maintained. Neighbors, relatives, and co-workers are interrogated as lawyers search for insight about philosophical and political slants of the prospective jury members. The reason for surreptitious prying is simple: Knowledge is power. The more the lawyer knows about a juror prior to court, the less he needs to ask during voir dire. Pre voir dire is a game for the elite—average people can't afford this luxury. It's too expensive.

Although the concept of voir dire is to help find unbiased jurors, attorneys translate that to mean winners. Voir dire is a tool that makes winning possible when justice dictates otherwise.

While voir dire means to speak the truth, all the advocates seek from it is a panel of prejudice, hopelessly brainwashed to favor their client's position. Lawyers who claim that they use voir dire to build fair juries are either fools or liars. Attorneys have a duty to zealously represent clients within the bounds of the law. Since voir dire is legal, lawyers must use it by attempting to build a jury of bigots. Otherwise, the attorneys fail to zealously represent their clients. Lawyers are in a catch-22. The system they use defeats justice, but use it they must. Unless citizens come to the rescue, barristers will remain trapped in the quagmire of voir dire.

I believe there are only five necessary questions to ask of a juror:

1. Are you related to any parties, lawyers, or witnesses in this case?
2. Do you know any parties, attorneys, or witnesses involved with this case?
3. Have you made up your mind who should prevail in this case?
4. Will you base your verdict on statements made outside the courtroom that are not in evidence?
5. Will you let bias or prejudice affect your decision?

In an article about the hypocrisy of voir dire, Fahringer said, "Lawyers announce to the panel that they want only jurors who will decide the case impartially, while, in fact, they want partisan jurors." He further asserted that the jurors see through this deception: "We [the lawyers] lie to them and they in turn to us; this is a bad beginning for a project designed to discover the truth."

Prospective jurors are repeatedly asked, "Will you be fair and impartial?" The question is asked in such a manner that jurors know that they must answer in the affirmative. Once I heard a woman say "no." The obvious error of her answer was shown by the hush that fell over the courtroom. The judge then assisted the lady by asking her which party she would treat unfairly. Noticeably embarrassed, the woman stated that she would be fair. This force-feeding of continuous requests for impartiality commits the jurors, allowing counsel to argue at the close of the case that each juror promised to be fair.

In some jurisdictions, the judge conducts *voir dire* and asks the prospective jurors anywhere from a few to many questions. Lawyers perform the task in other jurisdictions. In federal courts, the questioning can be done by either the judge or the lawyers. The rules of federal court procedure encourage judges to permit some voir dire. When lawyers conduct voir dire, they devour court time. Advocates nuzzle up to the panel with painted-on smiles as they ask apparently innocuous questions such as: "Do you think you can be fair and impartial in this trial?"

The translation of this question has been discussed in length before, but the purpose of it is to secure a promise from the juror to be fair. This promise is later used most masterfully in closing argument to lay guilt on the jurors for their thoughts about either party.

Another favorite is: "Have you ever served on a jury before?" This loaded question smacks of unfairness. It appears to be asking, "Are you experienced, and therefore would you be a better-qualified juror?" The inquiry actually concerns a juror's gullibility. A new juror is ignorant and can be educated by counsel to view the law most favorable to the attorney's client. The purpose of the question is to determine the level of naïveté of the juror. It could be phrased, "Are you stupid enough to buy this story?"

During the voir dire process it is impossible to tell whether a juror is being candid. The people in the jury pool come in two basic categories: Those who want to serve and those who wish to avoid the duty. Interrogating jurors is going to elicit various responses depending upon whether the person wants to serve on a jury. Unfortunately, the replies of the prospective jurors will vary in honesty depending upon their agenda. *Nightline* asked attorney Sam Burstyn about jurors' veracity in the William Kennedy Smith trial. Sadly, he said that we never know when a juror lies on voir dire.

Fahringer related that when a juror wants to be on the panel, the answers given will be colored to favor selection. In the back of any juror's mind is the peremptory challenge, and if they want to be on the jury, they say what the lawyer wants to hear. Bias is difficult to uncover; a person who harbors hatred for a particular race or group of people is unlikely to proclaim that publicly. Their desire to serve causes them to give what they consider socially-acceptable or politically-correct statements. Lawyers must therefore sift through the misrepresentations to uncover prejudices of the jurors.

The assertion was brought home in a highly publicized murder trial. A private survey showed that 71 percent of the community who were eligible for jury service had made up their minds about the defendant's guilt. However, during skill-ful voir dire by counsel only 15 percent of the jurors admitted any form of predisposition. This shows the possibility that jurors lie to get on a panel.

The entire process is based upon deceit. Attorneys for both sides scream for a fair and impartial jury. But who's kidding who? This is totally illogical—a canard of huge magnitude. Of course what they really want is a jury that favors their position. They want a team of people who will vote for their client.

Stereotyping The Jury

Our process of jury "rejection" allows the lawyer to mold and shape the panel into a favorable group that behaves ex-actly the way the lawyer wants it to act. Opposing counsel resists this effort, attempting to offset it and steer the jury in an opposite direction. There are some specifics that attorneys follow: Defense attorneys want a panel that is sensitive to the plight of the oppressed and distrustful of authority, such as young people. Prosecutors look for law-and-order buffs, such as senior citizens, who believe that criminal behavior is out of hand.

In *Anatomy of a Jury* by Seymour Wishman, the author revealed that critical issues are: occupation, race, religion, and nationality of the jurors. Some prominent criminal defense attorneys stay clear of jurors with German or Russian back-grounds because they tend to be law-and-order-type citizens. In *Verdict* by Morris Bloomstein, we find that Scandinavians and Englishmen are also avoided by the defense for the same reason.

Prosecuting attorneys have a different list of nationalities that they dislike. These include any members of minority or oppressed groups. According to Bloomstein, they avoid "...the underdog and the underprivileged, Irish, Italians, Jews, French, Negroes, people of Spanish-speaking ancestry and those of Balkan heritage..." Another author disclosed in her book, *Juries on Trial*, that a handbook used to train prosecutors in Dallas County, Texas, contained racist ideas. Paula DiPerna relates part of the 1973 manual as stating:

> You are not looking for a fair juror, but rather a strong, biased and sometimes hypocritical individual who be-lieves the Defendants are different from them in kind, rather than degree; you are not looking for any member of a minority group which may subject him to oppres-sion—they almost always empathize with the accused.

This means that the prosecution wants a bigoted person who is disassociated from criminal defendants. Blacks, His-panics, Native Americans, gays, and people who fall into oppressed minorities for any reason are to be avoided. Pros-ecuting attorneys, who are sworn to uphold justice and be fair-minded, commonly expel jurors because of race, stacking the deck by pruning the jury of minorities. Isn't it obvious? The last thing a prosecutor wants is a fair juror.

What's Good For The Goose...

Bloomstein claims that if a prosecutor wants a particular type of juror in a criminal case, the same type of juror is also desired by the *defense* in a civil trial. And likewise, a good criminal-defense juror is sought after by civil-plaintiff lawyers. The importance of this is that lawyers are screening out jurors for ethnic backgrounds in both civil and criminal matters.

Lawyers don't stop at racial discrimination. They cull the jurors because of occupation, too. This chapter started with a showing of how well teachers do (or rather, *don't* do) in the selection process. According to Bloomstein, many criminal-defense attorneys seek entertainers, bartenders, waiters, and waitresses. The civil-suit plaintiffs also like the same group. From this it can be inferred that prosecuting attorneys and civil-suit defenders avoid these professions.

Prosecutors look for military retirees, civil servants, insurance company employees, and farmers. Wishman asserts that prosecutors are also looking for male Republicans, prosperous people, bankers, engineers, and accountants, while the defense looks for female Democrats, poorer people, social scientists, and members of minorities.

Clearly, all the statements about desires for a jury in the above paragraphs are generalities. They conform to the general wisdom, or lack thereof, of the members of the bar. Certainly there are exceptions. Clarence Darrow, famous for his defense in the monkey trial, liked to have Englishmen on his juries. The generalities discussed above would imply that people of English extraction would be prone to side with the prosecutor. Darrow reasoned that the English are capable of standing up for their rights even if they are in the minority. What Darrow was looking for was that one person who might cause the jury to *hang* (or fail to reach a verdict). This is a common defense tactic. When the state's case is so powerful that the defense has little chance of winning, they attempt to thwart justice by creating a jury that can't come to a decision.

Tainting The Pool

Earlier in this chapter, I told you that the pool from which jurors are drawn must be a "fair cross section of the community." The U.S. Supreme Court has held in several cases that this pool need not be a mirror image of the community, and acknowledged that it would be impossible to have proportional representation in a society as diverse and heterogeneous as ours. It is as wrong to include a racial group as it is to exclude them, according to the court.

But just because the jury pool is properly proportioned, that certainly doesn't mean the jury itself will be. Only a few from the pool will be selected for a particular case, and then, only the six (or twelve) who make it through voir dire, survive peremptory challenges, and avoid challenges for cause will actually get to stay and hear the case in the courtroom.

It's there that discrimination on a massive scale takes place. In American courtrooms, the equal-protection rights of the jurors are trampled upon and ferociously bludgeoned. With the blessings of the trial judge, people are rejected solely for fitting into the wrong group. In our courts they find that skin color, sex, height, or some other characteristic will cause their ceremonial dumping into the waste bin of useless jurors. In spite of our laws, history clearly shows that prosecutors bump minorities off juries.

Our Supreme Court has upheld this practice where it was shown to be of an egregious magnitude. In *Swain v. Alabama,* a 19-year-old black man was convicted by an all-white jury for raping a 17-year-old white girl and given a death sentence. The prosecutor struck all six black jurors peremptorily. In the county where the trial took place this was the common practice. Because of this, no black persons had served on a jury trial in 15 years prior to this case. Swain argued that he was denied equal protection. Surprisingly, the court held that systematic discrimination was not shown. The court said, in effect, go ahead and throw those spitballs. We will turn our heads away, even if a black person never serves on the jury, if you follow the correct legal procedure.

With this kind of decision coming from the court, prosecutors will continue to challenge people for race. Studies have shown that prosecutors regularly challenge jurors because they are black, but not when they are white. However, other studies have shown that conviction rates dropped in several areas when more blacks served on the jury panels.

Herein lies a tremendous problem. Lawyers must follow the Code of Professional Responsibility in every case. Under the dictates of the code, prosecuting attorneys must represent their clients competently and zealously within the bounds of the law. The prosecutors' clients are the people of the state or city and it is their duty to make the streets safe. It is their job to get convictions. They must believe that every defendant on trial is guilty, or they must dismiss the case. If they think that black jurors will let more guilty persons go free, then they might perceive a duty to exclude blacks from the jury panels.

Thankfully, the Court later overruled a portion of the *Swain* decision, but it was a timid step. They acknowledged that while peremptory challenges have no constitutional standing, they enjoy a long history in the common law. This means that the Constitution does not give lawyers the right to tear apart a jury panel at will. However, it has been an accepted practice for centuries.

When the Supreme Court decided *Batson v. Kentucky,* they scolded prosecutors for abusing the challenge system. The court made it easier for a defendant to allege discriminatory practices in jury selection. Unfortunately, enforcement of the new rule is nearly impossible. The district attorney can comply by stating a neutral reason for rejecting the minority members from the jury. In other words, a lawyer can dismiss a black juror as long as the lawyer can give the appearance of a valid reason for it. If an attorney is unable to think up a proper excuse for the rejection, that counselor is short on imagination.

While the prosecutors are good targets because of all the evidence against them, they are not alone. Defense attorneys are equally guilty. In civil and criminal trials, jurors are capriciously bumped. Often it is because of skin color or sex. Melvin Belli prefers men on the panel. He said, "Women jurors are too brutal." We either want a cross section of our community on the jury, or we do not. As long as the peremptory challenge is given arbitrarily to the lawyers, we won't see representative juries.

Justice Thurgood Marshall wrote a *concurring opinion* to *Batson*. A concurring opinion is not law. When a judge writes one, he is pointing out how he wanted the court to rule. In a scathing attachment to the case, Marshall pointed out that: "Misuse of the peremptory challenge to exclude black jurors has become both common and flagrant." He then listed several case histories from Missouri, Louisiana, and Texas where the abuse is particularly bad. He cited the instruction book of the Dallas County prosecutor's office where "any member of a minority group" is to be eliminated. An earlier version of the book instructed the prosecutors as follows:

Do not take Jews, Negroes, Dagos, Mexicans or a member of any minority race on a jury, no matter how rich or how well educated.

Justice Marshall went on to say that the right to have a fair and impartial jury outweighs the use of historically-accepted peremptory challenges. He realized that attorneys can't monitor themselves in this matter and that they will continue to reject jurors because of race. The Justice noted that prosecutors could invent neutral reasons for bumping all blacks off the panel. He said that it might even come from unconscious bias that is applied in good faith. Finally, Marshall asserted that we also must bar defense lawyers from using this tool, but said there was no possible way to check this abuse, save elimination of the right to challenge peremptorily.

While most of the evidence of lawyer abuse of their absolute challenge privileges regards race, it also occurs because of sex, occupation, age, and marital status. The law says that discrimination is illegal, but it is a law that can't be enforced in jury selection.

Interestingly enough, Justice Marshall was replaced by Clarence Thomas, who wrote a concurring opinion to a follow-up case of *Batson*. In it he concluded with the following:

> I write separately to express my general dissatisfaction with our continuing attempts to use the Constitution to regulate peremptory challenges... I doubt that this departure will produce favorable consequences. On the contrary, I am certain that black criminal defendants will rue the day that this court ventured down this road that inexorably will lead to the elimination of peremptory strikes.

Here we see the difference between a conservative black justice and the liberal one. Thomas wants to keep things as they were by protecting the lawyer's right to peremptorily challenge jurors. Marshall saw a need for change and pledged to correct the problem. If you think, like Justice Thomas does, that the jury selection system is acceptable, then you will likewise allow the lawyers to stack juries favorable to their clients. Should you possess some of the vision of Justice Marshall, you know that it's wrong to discriminate against jurors because of their color or creed.

Summing up this section, we find that lawyers lie to the jurors about wanting an unbiased panel. The jurors in turn lie to the attorneys about their prejudices so they can get selected for the trial. All of this lying takes place under the guise of voir dire. After the lying is done, the lawyers slice the heart from the panel with their peremptory challenges, which is merely sanctioned discrimination, leaving only a shell of the original panel.

CHAPTER 3

Presumption Of Guilt

Parties fight lawsuits in both criminal and civil courts. The main distinction between the two types of litigation is the result: criminal convictions rip liberty from the defendants while civil verdicts extract their money. There's also a difference in the level of proof required to snag the prize.

Civil cases need a *preponderance of the evidence* on one side before a party can prevail. From this level of proof comes the famous Lady of Justice who holds a scale in her outstretched hand as she metaphorically weighs the evidence. To assure the hearing is fair and impartial, she wears a blindfold. When the case opens, both sides of the scale are empty and in balance. Even a breath of proof tips the scale. During the trial, evidence flows to one side or the other, tossing the scale out of equilibrium. The teeter-totter oscillates as the parties shoot arrows and hoist shields. Bloodied and bludgeoned, the parties and their advocates halt the battle after all witnesses have testified and both sides have argued. At the conclusion, the Lady of Justice examines the scale; the side with the heaviest evidence snares the victory... or is supposed to.

A preponderance of the evidence is nothing more than a simple majority. That means that the best case should win. In theory, if half the proof lies with the defendant and half rests with the plaintiff, the jury will hang and be unable to reach a verdict. Should 51 percent slide over to either party, the weight is sufficient to tilt the scale and they win the case.

Criminal trials differ from their civil counterparts because of a tougher standard of proof. The prosecuting attorney is the plaintiff and must present proof *beyond a reasonable doubt* to win the case. This is a much higher standard than a preponderance of the evidence. If the state only has 51 percent of the proof, the defendant goes free. Evidence presented by the prosecuting attorney must tilt the scale decidedly. If the scale is in balance, or slightly out of level, the defendant wins. Often, the prosecuter proves the defendant is the culprit but loses because the proof failed to clear the reasonable-doubt hurdle.

Besides the high standard of proof that must be met in a criminal case, another legal nicety protects the accused. It's the shield of the *presumption of innocence*. The state must topple this barrier to convict the defendant by presenting some proof that the defendant is guilty. The presumption of innocence and reasonable doubt muck up many a prosecutor's dreams and ruin many perfect records. When used skillfully, these two procedural prophylactic devices protect more wretched crooks than an epidemic of jailbreaks.

These tools aren't without disadvantages. The presumption of innocence is an extremely difficult concept to show jurors who equate being charged or jailed with being a criminal. If they read about it in the newspaper, they think the allegations are sufficient to cast doubt on the accused. Wrong as it might be, this is a logical assumption. On the street, the ordinary citizen thinks that there's a presumption of guilt. Only in court are we forced to don the absurd fiction that defendants are angels before the trial starts. Many legal scholars agree that the police rarely arrest the wrong person. To them, the issue at trial isn't so much, "Did this person do the act?" Rather, it's,

"Is this act a crime?" If people actually were presumed to be innocent, then nobody would ever sit in jail awaiting a trial. The presumption is a fantasy, but skillful defense lawyers use it well.

To display the actual presumption, which is, one of guilt, consider the following case: I was defending a fellow charged with shoplifting. In the jury pool was a manager of a toy store from a local mall. When her number was drawn for the panel, I asked her a few preliminary questions. Then, I asked her, "If you saw my client in your store tomorrow, would you take any special precautions?" She openly admitted that she would watch all the mirrors the entire time, just in case he tried to steal again. This was before the trial; he hadn't been convicted. So much for the presumption of innocence. So much for that juror. I removed this juror, not with a peremptory challenge, but with one for cause—she was obviously biased.

A frequently asked question by defense attorneys is this: "Ms. X, do you agree with the statement that it is better to release ten guilty defendants than to convict an innocent one?"

If Ms. X says no, she's off the jury, bumped by the defense. If she says yes, even if she's lying, she starts thinking that it's better to clear a creep than to convict a choirboy. The juror begins her service on the defensive, more concerned about making a mistake than reaching the correct verdict. Basic psychology is at work clearing some guilty defendants.

When I question potential jurors, I will ask *one* of them the following questions to demonstrate the presumption of innocence. The sequence usually goes like this:

ME: Mr. Dence, Do you understand that Jerry is innocent until proven otherwise—that there is a presumption of innocence surrounding him?
MR. DENCE: I think so. (He hasn't a clue, as will be seen.)

ME: Do you agree that Jerry is innocent unless the state shows you differently? (I always put the word innocent near my client's first name. Likewise, I never use the word guilty when talking to jurors. I want them thinking of my client as a person, not some textbook criminal, and most importantly I want to associate innocence with him.)

MR. DENCE: *Yes.*

ME: I noticed that you answered rather emphatically. I take that to mean you totally agree with the concept of the presumption of innocence—that you don't look at it as a technicality, is that correct?

MR. DENCE: Yes.

ME: The fact that two police officers arrested Jerry doesn't take away that presumption of innocence, does it?

MR. DENCE: No.

ME: Will that presumption stay with Jerry even though he was unable to raise bail and has been in jail since the day he was arrested?

MR. DENCE: Yes.

ME: So, what you're saying is that Jerry is presumed innocent as he sits here in court, is that correct? (I'm purposely asking close-ended questions that can only be answered "yes" or "no." While I usually want the juror to talk freely, at this stage I only want to make the upcoming point. So, I put the words in his mouth.)

MR. DENCE: Yes.

ME: Suppose you're selected on this jury, and right now, before we hear any testimony, before the case begins, the judge sends you back into the jury room to deliberate. What verdict would you give? (As the reader, what is *your* verdict?)

MR. DENCE: I don't understand. We'd go back before we heard anything?

ME: That's correct. What verdict would you give?

MR. DENCE: I couldn't make a decision. I'd have to hear some evidence.

ME: But, Mr. Dence, haven't we just spent the last few minutes talking about the presumption of innocence?

MR. DENCE: Yes, but—I'd be unable to do anything. I wouldn't vote either way.

ME: If the state fails to put on any evidence, then the presumption must do *something*. What verdict would you give?

MR. DENCE: (The light brightens; he has a clue.) I guess I would vote "not guilty."

ME: I notice some reluctance in your answer. Jerry is presumed innocent. He is "not guilty" if the state doesn't overcome that presumption. Is there any doubt in your mind that if the state failed to produce any witnesses, failed to admit any evidence—that you would vote other than for acquittal?

MR. DENCE: I would vote for acquittal.

Did you answer the test correctly? By interrogating Mr. Dence, I lost him as a juror. He disliked me for making him look stupid. He pretended to understand the presumption. Had I left him alone, he'd have served on the jury and given the prosecutor a strong advantage. My client would be presumed guilty at worst, or at best, Mr. Dence would have dismissed the shield in criminal law that presumes everyone is innocent.

What he didn't understand, is that every juror on the panel would have answered almost the same way he did. Nobody had the slightest idea what the presumption of innocence was or how it affects a case. Although I didn't like embarrassing a juror, I had no choice. I had to show all of the other jurors that they must follow the presumption of innocence.

If I had wanted Mr. Dence to acknowledge the presumption of innocence, I would have asked him: "But, Mr. Dence, if you haven't heard any evidence that he's guilty, and you presume him to be innocent *before* the case begins, wouldn't you find him 'not guilty'?" But I couldn't lead Mr. Dence with such a direct question. He would have seen through my trap and answered "yes" without thinking.

Only a dormouse could have slept through my interrogation of Mr. Dence. After hearing it, the remaining jurors will pay lip service to the presumption of innocence. To be certain that the other jurors understood how important this presumption was to me, I used a peremptory challenge on Mr. Dence, bumping him off the jury.

While it seems unfair to sacrifice Mr. Dence, my client comes first. He's accused of a crime, possibly a very serious one. I can't take a chance that jurors will understand the presumption of innocence without using some shock therapy. With the average person on the street, a defendant is presumed guilty. I had to overcome this logical assumption that all the jurors had, and let them know that the trial begins with an important legal fiction. I can't allow jurors to be prejudiced by common sense. Sometimes, the presumption of innocence is the only arrow in my quiver. I won't give it up without a fight. The stakes are too high.

But in using it, I'm twisting the minds of the jurors—and that's why I don't like it. They become so obsessed and confused over the presumption of innocence that they unknowingly are leaning toward my client, even before testimony begins. I'm using the presumption of innocence as a red herring.

Baring a theoretical case where the state forgets to put on any evidence, the defense has some other advantages. To succeed, a defendant need only present enough evidence to take the edge off the plaintiff's case. Defendants win acquittals if they raise a reasonable doubt in the minds of the jurors as to the truth of the case. A criminal plaintiff must show much more than 51 percent to win a conviction.

This high standard of proof that prosecutors toil under leads many critics to say, "We have a system designed for crooks." My answer is: While it's true that in trial the defendant receives the benefit of most doubts, the entire system is far from defense-oriented. But more importantly, if *you* were on trial, isn't this the way you would want it to be?

The following example traces an imaginary criminal case:

Chugger stopped at a tavern after work and shared a few pitchers of beer with a friend. Glowing from the ale, he departed. As he left the pub, he stumbled and fell against Deputy Blue of the local sheriff's department. The pair tumbled to the ground. Blue's jacket sleeve ripped as they fell. The gang at the bar heard the commotion and ran outside, subjecting Blue to a few rude insults along with razzing. Two other deputies saw the struggle and raced to Blue's aid with pistols drawn. Jeers from the crowd ceased.

Officer Blue controlled the entire case at this point. He had total discretion to detain Chugger or let him go. The deputy could also have called for a wagon to pick up our drunken friend and transport him to a detoxification center. However, since Blue's pride was on the line, he decided to arrest Chugger and wrote a report recommending prosecution for assaulting a police officer.

The report landed on the desk of the prosecuting attorney, who evaluated the case and decided to take it to trial. Either he relied solely upon the police report or had other officers investigate the matter further. Since the prosecutor thought the case was solid, he filed it and sent a summons to Chugger, ordering him to appear in court to defend himself.

Chugger had no say in the matter of making the decision to prosecute. Now, he faces horrible odds, since three deputies are going to testify that he knocked Blue to the ground. His only chance is to convince the jury that he accidentally fell into the officer. The prosecutor must prove beyond a reasonable doubt that Chugger knocked the policeman down intentionally. Here's where the high standard of proof aids Chugger. If he raises a reasonable doubt that it was not intentional (an accident), he escapes punishment. Chugger need not prove he is innocent beyond a reasonable doubt. In fact, he can't do it. It's a foolish defense attorney who attempts to prove innocence. The lawyer would be giving up a great tactical edge by attempting to show the client to be blameless. Chugger must only cloud the case enough so that the jury is uncertain of his guilt. Should he raise a reasonable doubt, he avoids the prosecutor's snare.

Giving a defendant the benefit of the doubt has its downside for the accused. So little evidence is needed by the defense to discredit the prosecutor's case that one can't prove innocence. This is why our criminal system never exonerates a defendant. It only says that the proof failed. A verdict of "not guilty" isn't the same as a declaration of innocence. A criminal defendant can't receive a verdict of exoneration from a criminal court. He can only be released on the charges. His name forever carries the stigma of the trial and the shadow of suspicion.

Chugger was just an unlucky drunk who wandered into a deputy. Yet, he has no way of totally clearing his name. The arrest and trial will stigmatize him as a potential assailant. The adage attaches, "Once arrested, always suspected."

As the allegations against a defendant rise in severity, the shame increases. Reputed New York crime boss, John Gotti, faced charges of racketeering, assault, and attempted murder in three separate trials. He won acquittals in all three cases. Did that clear his name? Of course not.

The verdicts only made people sneer at the system. He earned the nickname "Teflon Don" for his ability to slide out of trouble. Prosecutors kept after him relentlessly. Many people believed that he got off on technicalities, or witnesses became reluctant, or jurors were bribed. Acquittals freed him, but he kept the reputation of a mobster. Finally, in 1992, the government put together a case that stuck to the don. He's serving a long sentence for ordering a murder.

Although Richard Nixon never faced a jury, he will always be suspected of being a crook because of allegations that were leveled against him. Even President Ford's pardon did not remove the stigma. If anything, the pardon gave Ford a stigma of his own. If Nixon had a full-blown trial and had been acquitted, he would always be distrusted.

Acquittals in the first trial of the police officers who bludgeoned Rodney King will be forever suspect in the minds of many, if not most Americans. Even subsequent acquittals for two of the officers in the second trial won't erase the stigma of these charges. Most people saw a two-minute video and knew something was grossly improper about the arrest. The "not guilty" verdicts didn't change public opinion about the Los Angeles Police Department. After the Persian Gulf War, *Tonight Show* host Jay Leno cracked a joke that says it best: "I know how to get rid of Saddam Hussein. We just send LAPD over there."

Our system is imperfect; it lacks a method to exonerate. It only allows defendants to escape punishment, but it never clears them. Once a person is accused, the cloak of criminality forever attaches.

After all, it doesn't take that much of a defense to raise a reasonable doubt of guilt. If the doubt is reasonable, the defendant ducks the charges. That's why we acquit so many guilty people. We purposefully set the standard of proof extraordinarily high to reduce the chance of convicting innocent people.

Hey, Diddle Diddle

Nowhere in criminal law does guilt cling more tightly to an accused person than in sexual abuse matters. An allegation of sexual misconduct falls into a deep crevice of our judicial system. While murderers and robbers who go free are looked down upon, sexual defendants are ostracized and forever bear the mark of a pervert, whether acquitted or convicted. We still brand our citizens with Nathaniel Hawthorne's *Scarlet Letter,* despite the outcome. Only the letter is changed, from "A" for adultery to "P" for pervert.

In civil law, if the defendant can tilt the evidence until most of it favors him, he wins the trial. However, he's still vanquished. Marred by the assault on his character, there always remains that cast of suspicion. As much as 49 percent of the evidence could have pointed toward guilt. The shroud of sexual perversion is a difficult blanket to shake. For all the good the trial did him, he might just as well stamp a capital "P" on his forehead.

In this manner, it's seen that our civil court system doesn't find guilt or innocence so much as say whose side has the better case. Who told the truth remains a riddle. Our system only resolves disputes, declares the victor, and punishes the vanquished. Judges are rarely certain that their decisions are perfectly correct.

To give the matter a little air, consider Woody Allen's case. He reportedly sued Mia Farrow for custody of their three children from the eleven years the couple had been together. Farrow responded with serious allegations of sexual abuse by Allen of the children.

For years, Allen has delighted movie watchers with characters who relish in sexual innuendo and erotic slapstick. In *Sleeper* he played a pseudo-spy who hid from the authorities by dressing up as a robot. While in the disguise, he got locked up alone in a sex booth called an orgasmatron as it cycled and recycled. While barely able to walk after the heroic ordeal, the smirk he wore adroitly presented full comedic relief. In a later movie, a character he played said words to the effect, "Some of the best sex I've had has been when I was alone." He made his living making people laugh at his sexual inadequacies àla Pee Wee Herman. Now he's facing the irony of having his stage characters brought into his personal life with Farrow's allegations of sexual deviancy.

Since this is a civil case, Allen must fight *without* protection from the presumption of innocence. Were it criminal, he'd have it as a shield and would need far less proof to show wrongful charging. All he would need to do is discredit Farrow's case ever so slightly and he would be acquitted. However, in civil court, he must prove by 51 percent that he's not a baby diddler.

Understandably, Allen vehemently denied the allegations. He was reported as saying: "[The accusations are] a currently popular though heinous card played in all too many child-custody fights." The reported quote went on: "These totally false and outrageous allegations have sickened me... This is an unconscionable and gruesomely damaging manipulation of innocent children for vindictive and self-serving motives." He also suggested that Farrow offered to stop an investigation for $7 million.

Allen's new lover, Soon-Yi Previn, Farrow's adopted daughter, defended Allen and asserted that her mother had a nasty temper. The *Associated Press* reported her to say that Farrow punched her, hit her with a chair, and ripped her clothing as Previn fled from the apartment. This supposedly occurred after Farrow learned of an affair between Allen and Previn. Proving that Farrow is explosive is beside the point. Having a foul disposition doesn't necessarily mean she would lie to get custody of children.

Farrow's lawyer, Alan Dershowitz, reportedly countered Allen's assertions: "[Allen has] his facts all wrong. Connecticut authorities initiated their investigation *before* Mr. Allen filed his custody suit... There was never any 'demand' by Ms. Farrow's lawyers for 7 million dollars or any other sum of money."

In the wake of all these cross-allegations, two of Farrow's other children reportedly supported the abuse allegations against Allen. To counter these, his lawyer then announced that Allen passed a polygraph examination "with flying colors." The director/actor's sister reportedly came to his defense, calling the charges reprehensible and suggested that Farrow made the accusations out of fear of losing the custody case.

Farrow ultimately won the custody battle, and Allen won the stigma. It will be there tomorrow, next year, next decade, until his name is erased from history. Though he may win in civil court, the stigma will forever scar him. No amount of proof could show he didn't molest the children. Not even recantations by the accusers would clear him. A person can't show the negative. To show a person did something, one needs only produce a witness who observed the activity. That's proving the positive. The negative, however, requires accounting for every second of a person's life to show it couldn't have happened. It's an impossible task. There will always be that suspicion. The tragic thing is, whether he is guilty or not, his reputation was indelibly marred by a single accusation. All of his wealth, power, and fame can't mount an adequate defense. The charge alone is so repulsive that people won't concern themselves with the veracity of it. We've grown not at all since Hawthorne wrote *The Scarlet Letter*.

Bust 'em

Like in civil court, criminal assertions of sexual misconduct are simple to make and impossible to disprove. Former boxing champion Mike Tyson knows this all too well. Never to be mistaken for a goody-two-shoes, he faced many sexual allegations in the legal mill. He won a couple of decisions, but was ultimately knocked out for the count.

Tyson's past is checkered with accusations. Most of them alleged fighting or sexual assaults. One such case appeared in *Jet*. It said that a woman sought $4.5 million in punitive damages from the boxer, alleging he grabbed her breasts and buttocks in a disco club. Tyson's attorney effectively argued: "You should send a message, ladies and gentleman. That message is, if [the plaintiff] wants to engage in a get-rich-quick scheme, she should buy a lottery ticket." She won the suit, but only $100 was awarded to her.

Others included a reported filing by the Miss Black America Pageant that named ten contestants who alleged that Tyson despoiled the pageant by sexually harassing the participants. The suit prayed for $607 million. Out of the same event, a former Miss Black America reportedly filed for $100 million against the ex-champ for grabbing her buttocks.

Another issue of *Jet* reported that the Pageant dropped its lawsuit against Tyson. The founder of the pageant, said they sued because of reports that Tyson was a "serial buttocks fondler." The founder allegedly said the suit was dismissed when "I discovered that several contestants... [who] stated that Mike Tyson had fondled their buttocks, were telling outright lies specifically for the purpose of obtaining publicity..." He then added that two women made a "brief career of lambasting Tyson and the pageant on national talk shows..." Hard as it is to imagine, some participants of the beauty contest apparently lied for fame, glory, and a shot at Tyson's pocketbook.

Dismissing the civil suit didn't end the boxer's troubles from the pageant. Another contestant, Desiree Washington, filed a criminal complaint of rape against Tyson instead of a civil suit. A grand jury indicted Tyson after a three-week inquiry. A trial followed. Overmatched and outclassed, Iron Mike got slammed with a six-year prison sentence.

Tyson's lawyers were criticized for presenting the "creep defense." Their case showed the boxer as a masher on the prowl. They reportedly argued that anyone at the pageant knew Tyson had only one thing on his mind.

Another aspect presented by the defense was that Washington was motivated by money. That argument worked for Tyson in a previous civil case. Finally, Washington was portrayed by the defense as a consenting adult who went to Tyson's hotel room at 2 a.m.

While there was medical evidence in the trial, it primarily came down to another "he said—she said" case. As with the Woody Allen/Mia Farrow allegations, someone must decide who lied. Washington reportedly testified: "My eyes were just filling up with tears. I kept saying, 'Please let me go.' And he just laughed—like it was a game." Tyson's testimony was reported to be in exact opposition. He stated in court, "I didn't violate her in any way… She never told me to stop. She never said I was hurting her in any way. She never said no."

The entire case rested on who was the most believable. Sexual charges are usually like this. The jury believed Washington and convicted Tyson, acknowledging that the state overcame the presumption of innocence. By convicting Tyson, it was as if the jury said in effect, "You haven't even raised a reasonable doubt in our minds that you did anything but assault Washington against her will."

The idealistic view is that truth will prevail. In court, however, the truth is practically irrelevant. What matters most is
how the case is presented. The side with the appearance of
candor takes the booty. Generally, the best actor wins.

Mark Shaw wrote a commentary for *USA Today* about
Tyson's case. In it he listed several lawyering errors by defense counsel. Included in the list of mistakes was one for
allowing an "unprepared" Tyson to testify at the trial. This
"unprepared" witness said "all the wrong things" both to the
jury and the judge. Maybe the writer would have been happier
if the defense attorneys had coached Tyson until he had his
testimony memorized and recited the lines like an actor in a
play.

What this means is that lawyers are wrong when they don't
coach their witnesses to say only the right things. A sad
commentary on our system, worsened only the more because
it's irrefutable. In court, the best actor often demolishes the
side of truth. With life, liberty, or money at stake, integrity
often rides in the rumble seat. Only two people in the world
know whether the verdict was correct, and neither of them
was on the jury.

Later events compounded the case. When Judge Gifford
sentenced the boxer to six years in prison, she denied him the
right to post bail pending his appeal. While the fighter served
time, events unfolded. Shortly after reporting to prison, Washington filed the anticipated lawsuit against Tyson for damages. Her lawyer was quoted as saying: "Mr. Tyson has begun
to repay his debt to society for the crime he committed. This
suit is about his obligation to Ms. Washington."

Suddenly, Washington comes across as being elevated from
the poor victim of a "date rape" to the lofty status of a
"money-seeking" plaintiff. Recall that when Tyson defended
an earlier suit he said the plaintiff was after the bucks and the

jury agreed. The tactic didn't work in the criminal trial because of a major difference in the two cases:

The previous case was a civil suit, which directly asked the jury for cash, so his attorneys effectively argued it was a money-grab scheme. In the rape trial this argument was ineffective because criminal cases don't ask for money from the wrongdoer. Washington didn't even file her civil case until after the boxer was convicted. Tyson couldn't credibly argue that the case was for money when none was being asked for at the time.

On The Beach

Yet another highly publicized "he said—she said" comes from Florida. At 3 a.m. in the Au Bar, 30-year-old Patricia Bowman sat until she met her knight. Not only did he come from a sterling background, but he was also about to become a doctor. According to her testimony, she never missed a chance to banter about her daughter's health problems when she met a physician socially. She had latched onto a prize, or so she thought.

After an hour or so in the bar, William Kennedy Smith and she allegedly traveled to the Palm Beach Kennedy-family compound in a Mazda. At the home she got a glimpse of Senator Ted Kennedy and took a stroll on the Atlantic beach with Smith. A perfect Hollywood setting unfolded. Glamour, riches, fame, and a medical student were all bundled into this pick-up from the bar.

What happened on the Kennedy waterfront has two rather divergent versions. The following is an account of Bowman's testimony. She claimed that they had kissed earlier, but there had been no invitations for sex. While walking on the beach, Smith transformed from a pleasant young man into Robert Lewis Stephenson's Mr. Hyde. He tackled her, slammed her to the ground, and ravaged her body with a semi-erect penis. As she protested and struggled, he told her to "stop it, bitch."

After the alleged attack, Bowman went into the house and called friends to come and get her. She allegedly confronted Smith, saying: "Michael, you raped me. How could you do that?" When he said his name wasn't Michael and denied it was rape, she said, "My friends are coming, and I'll call the police." He answered, "Nobody's going to believe you."

The other side of the liars' contest came from Smith. He alleged that she picked him up in the bar. Denying any wrong-doing, he reportedly testified that there were two sexual encounters, both without any violence. He asserted that he was a passive participant who was assisted in consensual sex by a partner. She unbuttoned his trousers, massaged him to ejaculation, and waited for him to go for a quick swim. On his return from the water, she guided his penis into her vagina for their second sexual episode. Everything went along fine until he mistakenly called her Cathie, at which point she became furious and told him to get off her.

Between these two stories, the jury saw textbook lawyering. A superb defense was countered by lackluster prosecution of a flimsy case. This time, instead of Washington outclassing Tyson, the Kennedy glamour crushed Bowman.

Anne Mercer, the friend who came to rescue the distressed damsel from castle Kennedy, brought along a boyfriend who allegedly stole an urn from the house. The intent was to prove they had been there, that they weren't making up the entire story.

When Mercer testified, Smith's lawyer introduced the urn and left it in front of her throughout the ordeal, allowing the jury to ponder the apparently pilfered pot. Then he dug into her about her appearance on the television show, *A Current Affair* and the $40,000 she received for her handiwork.

Then in a move of extraordinary brilliance, the state called Senator Ted Kennedy, as if he would be stupid enough to injure his nephew's case. When opened up by defense counsel on cross-examination, the senator stole the show, discussing the deaths of Robert and John. He quit after successfully reminding the jurors of numerous Kennedy tragedies.

The prosecution was outgunned. Its case disintegrated before the nation to generations of Kennedy class and moxie. What occurred on the surface had nothing to do with what went on in the background. Everyone saw select family members file into the courtroom to support their Will. What they didn't see was money thrown lavishly on the defense case as five private investigators worked months picking up tidbits to pry apart the state's case. Experts studied the body language of potential jurors for defense-oriented traits.

The state, attempting to convict with a fragile case from the onset, had limited resources. Their lead attorney had an excellent record for convictions, but she had been playing with unfair advantages before meeting the Kennedys. A prosecutor only has to go to trial with the cases she thinks are winners. She can plea-bargain away the tough ones. Also, the state has far more resources than the average defendant can muster. The result is that district attorneys win most of their cases. The deck is usually loaded with so many aces for them that they can't lose.

Moira Lasch, the state prosecutor, was criticized for being stiff and sour. Her style was trashed in *Vanity Fair*, *New York Magazine*, and *Newsweek*, among many others. Much of this criticism was unwarranted. Lasch probably is a good state's attorney. However, prosecutors have such an easy time that they seldom develop style, poise, and presence in the courtroom.

Style is unnecessary when you wrestle society's goons. Being on the side of righteousness is usually enough. Police honor them by sitting at their counsel table, just in case the jurors forget who the good guys are. Prosecutors go after killers, rapists, drug dealers, and all manner of scum. They wear the white hats. The jury, the citizens, the press, everyone roots for them in most cases. They rarely play before hostile crowds; in fact, the term home-court advantage has more to do with criminal trials than with basketball games. To crush their prey, most prosecutors need only sneer at defendants at appropriate times to seize a coveted conviction from the jury.

The result is they hit many singles, but perceive them as home runs through their distorted glasses. When they meet a real defense, like the one the Kennedys put together for Will, they learn that they're sadly outclassed. The playing field no longer tilts in their favor. They're little leaguers, whiffing pathetically when tossed major-league fast balls.

Lasch blundered by letting Ted Kennedy talk about the assassinations of Jack and Robert. It's totally irrelevant to whether Will raped Bowman.

The jury apparently couldn't accept the claim that Bowman allegedly took off her shoes and pantyhose in the car without having sex on her mind. They might have believed the hole in the crotch of the pantyhose was proof of fondling before arriving at the estate. They might have been overpowered by the Kennedy aura. In any event, they came back in just over an hour with a "not guilty" verdict. The short deliberation showed contempt for the prosecutor's case.

Did we learn who, if anyone, lied? Absolutely not. Did the jury? They were in a worse position than the average citizen. They didn't learn that Smith allegedly had three suspiciously-similar incidents with other women. Nor did they learn that Bowman allegedly mothered a child out of wedlock and ventured into an abortionist's office to terminate three separate pregnancies. Those niceties were kept from the jury because they were too prejudicial. It's feared that the trial wouldn't have been fair if jurors heard such dastardly truths. The rules of darkness controlled as the court refused to let jurors learn the entire case. So, like any other "he said—she said" battle, nobody learned the truth. But everyone knows who put on the best show.

Even after his acquittal, Smith is remembered as a rapist. A newspaper article demonstrated how Smith feels. He reportedly advised his friend, Eric Douglas, son of actor Kirk Douglas, about a misdemeanor charge the younger Douglas faced. "Eric, my family spent over $1 million on my defense and all anyone remembers is that I was involved in a rape. Nobody remembers I was acquitted." So much for the presumption of innocence. Once arrested, always suspected. Douglas reportedly took four days in jail rather than fight the charges against him.

In the aftermath of the verdict, privacy-seeking Patricia Bowman granted interviews to *Vanity Fair* and *Nightline*. This is the woman whose identity was protected by a blue dot that appeared on television screens as she testified. The interviews were supposed to clear her name, to tell the world she passed three polygraph tests and a voice-stress analysis, and then to close the book on her. However, five months later, it was reported that the recluse came out of the closet. She had become a victims' advocate and organized a seminar for National Victims' Rights Week. She's using her fame now, and is anything but private.

Capital Hill

Clarence Thomas wanted success. He climbed from poverty to become chairman of the Equal Employment Opportunity Commission. From there, he won a seat on the bench of a federal court of appeals, and finally, the president appointed him to serve on the United States Supreme Court. All that was needed to complete this fairy tale of rags-to-riches was confirmation from the U.S. Senate.

The stated purpose of the confirmation process is to find whether candidates are qualified to occupy a seat on the highest court in the land. In reality, it's political. It matters not a wit if the proposed justice is a good lawyer, but only how he or she will vote on critical issues.

Abortion is the hot topic today, so Thomas was asked repeatedly how he felt about *Roe v. Wade*, the case that cleared the way for pregnancy terminations. The senators didn't want to know if Thomas thought it was a poorly reasoned case or if it rested on sound legal logic. All they wanted to know is if he would overrule the case. If he would, he was—in the eyes of the liberal senators—totally unqualified. However, to conservative senators he would be improper material for the Court if he wouldn't overturn the decision, thereby allowing abortions to become illegal again.

The liberal senators wanted him out, not for his limited judicial experience, but for his conservative attitudes. Conservative senators wanted him in for his views, not his qualifications. And so, a war began.

Anita Hill was located by someone, somehow, some way. She complained of alleged sexual harassment she suffered from her boss, Clarence Thomas. The events occurred ten years earlier, but she'd remained silent, until the Supreme Court nomination. In exchange for her accusations to wrench the job from Thomas, she demanded anonymity. When it appeared that Thomas would be confirmed despite her allegations, Hill went on National Public Radio to spew her story. Not exactly the path one would expect from a person crying for anonymity.

An outcry erupted as the lurid voyage began. A hearing on the allegations unfolded before a national television audience. Everyone in the country could hear how Thomas reportedly asked her, "Who put the pubic hair on my Coke?" The nation heard about Thomas' alleged pornographic tastes and "Long Dong Silver" as CNN cameras rolled out the action and suspense.

It was another "he said—she said" case. However, this one took a bit of a twist. Thomas didn't agree with anything the woman offered, although he refused to listen to her testimony. He claimed ignorance to what Hill said, then denied it anyway. Unlike Smith and Tyson, who said, "Yeah, but, it was consensual," Thomas professed complete innocence. He said that Hill made everything up and he had no idea why.

A complete denial is the most untenable defense in law. Our society doesn't like to make decisions that proclaim one person is a total liar. The worst defense possible is to claim total innocence. Failure to admit to some wrongdoing troubles people greatly. While juries are quick to let a killer off who says, "I did it, but he threw a knife at me," they're reluctant to clear the same person who defends by saying, "I wasn't there, I'm being framed."

As the head of EEOC, Thomas must have known that a total denial was the worst defense. People think that where there's smoke, you better have a fire extinguisher. Thomas could have taken an easier tack by saying, "Maybe I suggested some things to Hill that were out of taste." After all, they worked at the EEOC. The office investigated cases like this. Thomas could have even said he remembered discussing a particular case with her in a professional atmosphere. He didn't. He indignantly clamored that she lied.

The "trial," if you could call it that, was conducted by our esteemed senators, who doggedly chided any witness that damaged their side. It wasn't a case of Thomas and Hill, it was a case of liberal versus conservative. The truth of the charges didn't matter to the Senate; all the members cared about was victory for their political bent.

While almost all of the commentators claimed one of the two lied, none could say who. Polls taken nationally showed that men and women believed Thomas over Hill by a two-to-one ratio. Most people believed what they wanted, hearing only what coincided with their political bias. The matter wasn't decided because of right or wrong, facts or fiction. It came about because of emotions. Nobody is any wiser about the truth. Like other "he said—she said" fiascoes, only two people know what really happened. Everyone else is their patsy.

Years later, Thomas remains one of the highest-profile justices in the nation. This isn't necessarily because of his scholarly opinions, but because of the intense notoriety that he received from the Senate's "dog and pony" show. The ordeal branded him with the presumption of guilt; he wasn't even given the "courtesy" of a criminal trial. The eventual Senate confirmation failed to cleanse him. However, his accuser is no longer an obscure professor of law. She was among *Glamour's* "Women of the Year," appeared on the cover of *Newsweek*, and her name will be forever emblazoned in history books.

Thomas carries a stigma; Hill carries a torch.

CHAPTER 4

Here Come Da Judge

Bend the knees, take it back nice and slow, keep your eye on the ball. That's it, now keep the head down— "Objection, your honor!" screamed the frantic lawyer. "That question is argumentative."

"Overruled," said the judge with a bit of syrup in his voice. He went back to the land of nod, leaving the badgered witness as fresh meat for the hungry attorney. *Head down, slow backswing, meet the ball. Whapp. Oh, capital drive—now, let's see, an eight iron to the green, or a soft seven? Use the seven. Now—head down, slow—* "Objection, your honor! Counsel asked the same question three times. The witness already answered it."

"Sustained," frowned the judge, promptly returning to his mental golf game.

Would you like your fate decided by a person who day-dreamed through your trial? Does it happen? Yes, regularly. Judges suffer from the same distractions anyone else does. Whether it's a golf game, a hunting trip, or an IRS audit, their heads get clouded by outside disturbances.

But it's not quite the same as the mechanic who tunes your car while listening to the ball game. Judges fall into the same critical category as surgeons, not mechanics, and are expected to give you their very best... all the time. Have you ever wondered on the night before your operation, "Gee, I hope my doctor tucks in early tonight. What if he had to work late. God, do you think he drinks!?"

A judge I know occasionally reads *Field and Stream* instead of listening to counsel's closing arguments. I discovered this accidentally by approaching the bench during a summation and saw tell-tale pictures of antlers and guns. His look reminded me of a fifth-grader who got caught reading *Spiderman* in class.

While judges have vast powers, they still suffer human failings. Though their buttocks rest in esteemed chairs, their minds often wander. It forces attorneys to creatively present cases so the hearing officer pays attention.

The judge who flipped in and out of his backswing didn't care what went on in the courtroom. The case was routine, perhaps for shoplifting an item from a retail store. I've seen these cases presented dozens of times to several different judges. Most often, the only issue in petty theft from a store is whether the person intended to steal or forgot to pay.

To discover whether the act was accidental or intentional, the court listens closely to everything *until* the magic words come from a witness: "The accused took the package of cigarettes (pepperoni, shrimp, or whatever), and hid it in his pocket." Once the judge hears that the goods were secreted, the intent to steal is proven. I've heard several judges admit this. After hearing the critical phrase, the judge sits on the bench playing mental golf, waiting for the case to end. He already did his job. He heard the necessary words to convict the defendant. Only a startling revelation would change the predisposition to find guilt, something strong and memorable, like chipping from a sand trap into the hole.

Excuse Yourself

Judges have blessed and plagued humanity for ages. When they are good, they are very, very good, but when they are bad, they are horrid. The ideal judicial model was presented by Socrates:

Four things belong to a judge: to hear courteously, to answer wisely, to consider soberly, and to decide impartially.

Socrates' wisdom is unimpeachable. Judges should be courteous, wise, sober, and unbiased. Some of these characteristics escape many of our judges. Our entire country suffers when egocentric players get into power on the bench. We need jurists with integrity who will admit their prejudices and disqualify themselves because of them. Great care must be taken in selecting magistrates. When mistakes occur, they should be easily correctable. Our system of judicial appointments and elections is deficient in both categories.

Consider a charge of shoplifting, an offense that often reaches our trial courts. Many judges have tunnel vision on this crime. They look for the secretion of the goods as the critical evidence to convict the defendant. It's logical. The court sees several larcenists each week, most of them pilfered a small item that they concealed as they left the store. They're guilty, almost regardless of their explanation for the behavior. Hiding the goods is enough to convict an innocent person. Prejudice blinds judges under these circumstances.

Prejudice is a strong word in today's language. It conjures up pictures of racial hatred and bigoted attitudes. Pretty, it ain't. But judges are like other people, hampered by weaknesses and predispositions.

Over the years, I've tried several petty theft cases. I can't remember winning one to a judge, except on a *technicality*. By that I mean I won the case because of a procedural fault in the case.

While judges might have dismissed some cases because the constables blundered, my clients didn't win on the facts. In other words, the judge protected their procedural rights, but didn't believe their cries of innocence. Conversely, I've never lost one to a jury. This record leaves me totally predisposed to having a jury hear shoplifting cases.

From my perspective, almost every judge who hears a shoplifting case should excuse themselves. Many magistrates should disqualify themselves because their bias is flagrant. Once the magic words are spoken—"He put the beef jerky in his coat pocket"—the case is over.

My advice to petty thieves is: "Never hide your pilfered goods. Carry them out of the store in your hands. The judge won't hear the magic words and might believe you." My advice to the blameless who get accused of shoplifting is: "Trust the jury. They're less prejudiced against you."

But some cases mandate a bench trial. Drug dealers, for example, have a better chance before judges, as do prostitutes. Judges see so many slimeballs that they aren't as turned off by them, and might give a fairer hearing than would a jury.

Certainly, we can't condemn all biases. Some innocuous ones fill my repertoire—like preferences for German shepherd dogs and blue shirts. In my practice, I've had several cases dealing with Native Americans. Because of favorable experiences in these, I tend to be pro-Indian on most matters. These inclinations probably wouldn't keep me from being fair in a trial.

However, a blinding intolerance I suffer from is total disdain for neighborhood animal poisoners. Vengeance could overcome me in such a case; fairness to a defendant charged with feeding arsenic to a boy's puppy is out of the question. I would never hear such a case as a juror or represent an accused unless ordered to do so. My predisposition of the matter would force me to root for the prosecutor and hope for a harsh sentence.

In my state, we had a case that I could never have worked on or decided impartially. A popular grey donkey named Pasado lived for years at Kelsey Creek Farm. One evening, some teenagers and young adults reportedly jumped the fence to the park and visited Pasado. After harassing the helpless donkey, an intruder tethered it to a tree by tying a hangman's noose around its neck. The "lark" continued as the culprits allegedly beat the burro for nearly an hour until he fell dead. When I think of the case, I envision cruel teenagers laughing and taunting the defenseless donkey as it pathetically brayed for a respite. The gruesomely sadistic acts disgust me so thoroughly that I couldn't listen to any reason in the case. I know it; I'm too prejudiced to be a part of it. Pity the poor judge who was a part of it. Then, ask yourself what kind of a judge would you like to see these kids stand in front of?

The reported sentences for the participants were published in an article in the *Seattle Times*. A juvenile received 30 days detention and 200 hours of community service. An adult was sentenced to nine months in jail; another adult received a one-month sentence. I have to admit that I would have punished them more if I had been the judge. However, as I stated earlier, I would have excused myself from the case as too prejudiced to fairly judge it.

Now consider what the same article had to say about the sentencing judge. The prosecutor reportedly asked for exceptional sentences in the case. In Washington State, the courts follow sentencing guidelines, and judges only go outside the guidelines when there are exceptional circumstances. The judge declined to treat the case as an exceptional one. To me, I can't imagine more extraordinary circumstances than beating a donkey to death.

Further, the judge was reported to have blasted the prosecutors in the case for lacking "intellectual integrity" by asking for harsh punishment of the donkey killers. The judge reportedly intimated that the prosecutor wanted the punishment because of strong public sentiment against the assailants. The judge had reportedly received over 100 letters from the public asking for harsh sentences.

Earlier in the day, the same judge had reportedly sentenced a man for kidnapping and assaulting a 16-year-old girl. The victim had been abducted, beaten, disrobed, slashed with a knife along her throat, and discarded in a dumpster, apparently left for dead. Amazingly, the victim survived. The judge was quoted as saying:

> This court did not receive one letter from a member of the public urging the imposition of an exceptional sentence in that case (the attack on the girl)... I wish the public could demonstrate the same level of community indignation and concern for that 16-year-old girl as it did for Pasado (the donkey).

I have no doubt that the judge was sincere in trying to say that we care more for burros than we do for people. But looking deeper, what the judge described is a concern that elected officials—like judges and prosecutors—have with our system. They must answer to the people who elect them. Our government is a republic in which the majority is supposed to rule. Public officials must at least pay lip-service to their constituents. Sometimes the majority position is bigoted and morally wrong; however, I don't see how it can be morally wrong to side with a helpless donkey. When the majority is wrong, we need tough officials to stand up to them and do the right thing. No one ever said being a judge was an easy job.

The Jaundiced Eye

Because of the horrible connotation of the word "prejudice," people, and especially jurors, deny having it. This makes it difficult to uncover the latent biases. It's worse with judges. Their intolerances are only learned over time, and at great expense to lawyer's clients.

No discussion of prejudice would be complete without bringing up racial issues. The first thing that comes to mind with the word "prejudice" is racial disdain. People are so afraid of being labeled "bigot" that they run from the word. Nobody dares say anything remotely connected with African-American lifestyles for fear of being branded for unfairly stereotyping the whole class of people. Paranoia overtakes reason and the thought of prejudice is *verboten*.

As a telling example of how unreasonably frightened people are of the label of prejudice, Rush Limbaugh overreacted when Bill Clinton jokingly implied that the rotund talk-show host might have a tinge of racial prejudice. President Clinton was referring to how vigorously Limbaugh defended Attorney General Janet Reno from zealous quizzing by a black legislator. Limbaugh went on a tirade, announcing in program after program that "I'm not a racist."

The following statement is my opinion, based upon observations over some four decades. It has no empirical data to support it because to the best of my knowledge, there isn't any:

I believe that intellectual differences in groups are minor, and therefore imperceptible even under scrutiny. Red, white, yellow, and black skin pigmentations have little to do with intellectual performance. It's obvious that there are talented people of all colors. That's why I'm willing to learn about the fine line that distinguishes races.

Most people can accept the truth, if told it. It doesn't matter if we find out that women make better doctors or that blacks make better lawyers or that there is absolutely no difference in sexes and races. However, it's illogical that sexes and races are equal. Nothing else in nature is perfectly balanced; why would these be?

Prejudice is best described as an irrational belief, not based upon the facts. How can we learn the facts if we won't discuss them? Let's accept that we all have biases, try to discover whether they are based upon myth or fact, and go on from there. A philosopher once remarked that prejudice was never reasoned into anyone and can't be reasoned out of them. With open discussion, maybe we can prove that the sage was wrong.

Judges are predisposed in many areas and they need to face it. They're human—experiences shaped their beliefs. They're prejudiced against blacks, whites, women, men, gays, dogs, owls, Catholics, and an unlimited number of other things. If a judge is frightened to walk the streets at night because of gang members or drug dealers, he will have a tough time being fair when one appears before him. If a judge's brother is a logger, the Sierra Club could be in trouble when it presents a case. If a judge's daughter was killed by a motorcyclist, local bikers might be wise to avoid that court.

In the last two cases, you would obviously expect the judge to excuse himself, admitting to the potential bias. But what about the first example? No judge wants to admit he's afraid to walk his dog at night.

We need judges who have enough self-esteem and honesty to say: "I can't be fair." Magistrates must have the guts to admit petty prejudices. When they do confess to predispositions, they should be honored, not humiliated. It shouldn't be a blight on their record, but a commendable attribute that they refused some cases.

Leadership toward open discussion of bias should come from the bench, but judges with courage to admit intolerances are scarce. Since they rarely admit to prejudices, it's the job of the lawyer to know of these and effectively combat them. Lawyers must be quick to say, "I'm sorry, your honor, but I don't think that you can be fair with this case."

One of my first cases was before a jovial old gentleman in District Court. As I waited to try my client's case for driving while intoxicated, I chuckled at his folksy mannerisms and talk of "frontier justice." He was fond of reminding people charged with auto theft that "It wasn't long ago that we hanged horse thieves in this county; isn't car theft a lot like horse stealing?"

m' Lord

To the world, judges are the good, the trusted, and the impartial group of people who solve prickly issues for society. Their black robes flow over three-piece suits or chic dresses, and what you see is often different from what you get. When magistrates enter their domain, everyone rises to show respect, or possibly their fear. Their position and presence commands respect. If someone forgets the awe the venerated office demands, an army of bailiffs persuades a remembrance.

When they sit in judgment, they possess the power of God, the wisdom of experience, and the prejudice of fools. Judges do a most respectable public service: wash the country's dirty laundry.

Like other public servants, most are dedicated, trying to do their jobs well. Also, as with other government employees, their job security is of paramount concern. Judges don't want to be unemployed any more than a clerk does. Their jobs are their lives, in every way. They hold them tightly and many bad judges fiercely cling to their gavels.

Off The Bench

When a young man entered a courtroom, he expected punishment for disorderly conduct and public drunkenness. Little did he believe the court would offer leniency, but that's what happened. The judge said that if he could shampoo the young man's hair, he would get a break. Further, should he bring along some friends for a wash and rinse, even more judicial favor would be curried. The accused later appeared with two friendly plain-clothes state troopers who reportedly arrested the judge after their hair dried.

At least now we know why defendants were ordered to remove their hats in his courtroom.

Showing how terrible this abuse of authority can get, consider a judge who presided over juvenile matters. He would have adolescents assist him in reaching sexual climaxes in exchange for leniency. At least those were the allegations by several of his past defendants. In the wake of the charges, the judge shot himself dead.

Jet ran an article about a noble judge. He became a United States District Court Judge in the Deep South, an accomplishment for a black man. Alas, the esteemed judge went astray.

A convicted drug smuggler decided to turn informer. The shift occurred for anticipated leniency; however, our justice department didn't shampoo the smuggler's hair, they shaved his accomplices. The smuggler-turned-good-guy told the authorities about a businessman who was bribing him. Mr. Smuggler convinced the FBI to front him $100,000 in marked bills that were in turn tendered to the businessman.

Somehow, the judge acquired $16,500 of the marked bills. The businessman had a big chunk of the money in his possession. A jury convicted the judge of bribery, conspiracy, and obstruction of justice. Since the delightful judge received a lifetime appointment to the bench, he will remain on the public payroll unless Congress impeaches him.

Sometimes our judges are just too honest for their own good. In these days of annoyingly careful speech, even judges fall prey to their own tongues. *Jet* reported that a Southern judge showed his true bias by referring to black people: "We have been too good to them. They're the ones committing the crimes." He said that the district had enough black judges and needed more Jewish jurists who could work over the Christmas holidays.

A judge from the Midwest reportedly said that he'd only allow abortions to white girls raped by black men. Under a state law, minors seeking abortion need permission from a parent or a probate judge. Even though the judge later apologized, he was censured by the highest state court for misconduct in office.

Another flaky judge ordered a dress code for women in his courtroom. Their skirts, he said, can be no more than one inch above the knee, and no longer than mid calf. The *Associated Press* quoted him on the reasoning behind the order: "People were complaining to me wanting to know what country they were from, India or wherever." Sounds like a case of judicial tolerance at its finest and a clear signal for lawyers and their clients to discard any Nehru jackets left over from the '60s.

And still another story of a trial judge who can't shut his mouth. He reportedly told a lawyer in open court that he looked as though he had sexual relations with a bobcat in a phone booth. Then he was said to have made an ethnic slur toward the Iraqis during the Persian Gulf War. Keeping with diversified offenses, he was also reported to have told an indigent defendant "there are not many starving people. There's a lot of them too stupid to cook what they are given but nobody is starving." Finally, he touched on gay rights by allegedly explaining to an attorney that a defendant "had gone crazy" from too many homosexual encounters.

Imagine the justice a poor, gay, Arab would receive from this clown.

Court records show that a West Coast judge probably takes all awards for crass behavior and sexual harassment, despite what Anita Hill has to say. He was hearing a criminal case when he had the attorneys for both sides come into his chambers. In the conference, the judge pulled out a battery-operated "dildo" and thrust it toward the defense counsel's buttocks.

Later, in court, the defense attorney was cross-examining witnesses when the court implied that he should cut off the cross-examination or he'd get the "dildo" in open court. In the afternoon, the judge threatened him with a super-charged 15-volt model that had a longer handle. Again, defense counsel ceased cross-examination to avoid the embarrassment of being shown the Energizer Bunny's Revenge.

Lest one thinks that only the few people inside the robes do improper things, examine some of these extra-judicial acts. A *Washington Post* article portrayed the Ninth Circuit Court of Appeals as being fraught with sexual misconduct. Sixty percent of the female attorneys reported that they had been "the target of unwanted sexual advances or other forms of sexual harassment" by lawyers, judges, clients, and personnel of the appellate court. Six percent of the female attorneys accused judges of the unsavory conduct.

In Kansas, a judge was accused of having sex in his chambers with a female employee, and demanding it from another employee. The continued sexual relations were necessary for the women to keep their jobs. When one woman stopped complying, she was fired.

Dirty-old men flourish on the bench. An Eastern judge liked to play the field. He had a 21-year-old woman appear before him on four counts of worthless checks. After court, the judge allegedly followed the woman's car and had her pull over to speak to him. She got into his car and he asked how badly she wanted an attorney appointed. Was it a friendly inquiry, or a play for sex? The act of following her car raises many ethical questions.

The woman had another encounter with the judge at his behest; again in his car he tried to kiss and embrace her. The judge, who had power over the woman's future, recklessly abused his authority.

But striking out with the first was apparently unimportant. Another young woman appeared before him on a charge of driving while under the influence of intoxicating liquor. This time the judge allegedly went to the defendant's house unannounced and attempted to fondle her breasts and kiss her while simultaneously pushing her onto a bed. When the second woman resisted the assault, the valiant judge told her that he'd return the next day for round two.

As an aside, the judge was said to have presided over his own traffic infraction case and pressured the prosecutor into dismissing it.

Helping lift the awareness of "frontier justice," a judge resigned from the bench after playing "Dirty Harry" on the streets. It was reported that as the judge drove down a rural road, a vehicle passed him. His Honor thought the driver's actions were dangerous, so he repassed it, parked his truck, and attempted to stop the unsafe driver. Wisely, the driver of the van ignored the judge's demands. At this point our judge allegedly pulled out a handgun and fired at the vehicle. The magistrate said he wanted to hit a tire. Luckily, he missed everything.

No, it doesn't only happen in California. Court records show that in New York a judge went to a tavern and confronted several black patrons. His true feelings came out as he badgered them with racial slurs and warned them never to come into his courtroom. The police responded twice before ridding the inn of the bar-room bigot. New York's Court of Appeals jerked him from the bench.

A judge was reported to have flipped a coin to decide a traffic infraction in open court! The accused called heads, but the quarter landed tails.

The judge was quoted as saying: "You have to have a sense of humor... he said he never speeds. The officer said he did. I said I'd give him the benefit of the doubt—a 50-50 chance."

The judge's behavior and statements are appalling. They show total lack of regard for judicial decorum and legal understanding. If he were truly giving a defendant the "benefit of the doubt" he would have dismissed the case. However, this judge apparently labors under the "presumption of guilt" instead of the "presumption of innocence."

Sentencing for Life

Judges need some controls slapped on them. When they preside for years, some get better, others become bored and stale. A few of them turn into tyrants. Unsuspecting litigants grovel before judges who play mental golf and flip coins to decide matters.

Under the Constitution, federal judges are politically appointed for life. The party in power loads the courts with right-thinking jurists whose philosophy reflects that of the administration. This causes considerable strain on our blindfolded lady. Consider when Ronald Reagan was president. Jurists seeking promotion knew that they had to oppose abortions. This affected decisions coming from the benches across the nation. Justice suffered to please the boss.

Reagan isn't the only president who stacked courts with proper-thinking judges. A person hoping for a position on the bench under Johnson's presidency could discard any conservative views. The system of administrative appointments shows the good ol' boys at work.

When a person gets on a federal bench, they are next to impossible to remove. It literally requires an act of Congress to impeach a judge. Anyone who viewed the Judge Thomas confirmation process knows that the members of the Senate couldn't agree whether to eat popcorn with their left hand or their right. They can't halt their gridlock to remove the impaneled judges. Impeachments are about as rare as midnight solar eclipses. It's safe to say that barring idiocy and rampant corruption from the bench, it's impossible to remove a federal judge.

Unfortunately, change is probably not in the offing. Our Founding Fathers wrote the Constitution to protect federal judges. It makes them gods for life. Congress isn't going to do anything about the situation; at least it hasn't yet.

It would require a constitutional amendment to change the federal situation. With pressing issues of the deficit, the economy, world peace, nuclear disarmament, racial tension, uncontrolled litigation, and environmental protection to hide behind, Congress won't end its gridlock to correct its flawed judicial selection process. The senators are too proud of how they handled the Clarence Thomas nomination to want change. I can't imagine that a drive to limit judicial terms would build enough steam to become law. Our Senate must enjoy playing court jester to convicted felons who still collect their salaries. If anything is ever to change in the judicial selection process, it must start at the local levels, where a citizen has some chance of being heard. Our federal government won't change, and the citizens have no vehicle to make it happen.

When bums get on the bench, it must be easy to fire them. There's little argument for keeping convicted felons, thieves, bullies, or pigs on the payroll. Forget the federal courts. The Congress controls them, and barring an outcry louder than ever heard before, the legislature will continue to gripe and refuse to act.

Choosing Sides

Most of our states have developed a different manner of judicial selection from the federal monstrosity. Some governors appoint judges. That's more of the good-ol'-boy choosing like the federal government model. Other states fill positions by election for a term of years, but not for life. Voters of the district decide who will sit as judge.

In theory, bad jurists could be recalled in the middle of their terms, or they could lose when up for re-election. In reality, recalls are scarce enough to disregard. Having elections takes care of the good-ol'-boy syndrome, but it has enough drawbacks to fill a dozen inside straights.

Instead of playing to the boss, judges pander to the electorate. Their decisions must be in line with public opinion or they may have to go back to work in a law firm. People who want to be elected judges aren't as concerned with political connections as they are with popularity.

Cases involving criminals are loaded with prejudice. Tough sentences win votes, even when imposed on innocent defendants. Everyone wants to be tough on crime today—whatever the cost.

A sitting trial judge in a recent election running for appellate court, took out radio ads that proclaimed how harshly he treated a child molester and how frequently he exceeded the guidelines to give tougher sentences to criminals. Another thing he explained in the ads was how he made it possible for people to sue their employers for extra money.

This ad might suggest that some judges are tempted to pander justice to achieve promotions. When someone goes into court, their case is the only one that is supposed to be considered, and in a vacuum, not with an eye on a re-election bid. This problem will plague us until judicial elections are banned or reformed.

Next, the ability of the electorate to assess judicial qualifications needs discussion. The average person on the street has no basis whatever to discern judicial abilities. Many voters rely on the experts to guide them. They ask lawyer friends who would make a proper judge. It's sensible, except many attorneys never go to trial, and many of those who do lack understanding of the workings of court.

Ever notice who supports judges seeking election? Most frequently it's a group of lawyers. It makes sense, doesn't it? Lawyers should know more than anyone who's a qualified judge. Wrong. Having lawyers select judges is like letting the fans choose umpires. Attorneys are looking for judges who rule their way. They don't want fair trials; they want victories. Lawyers are too biased to choose judges. Allowing them to pick our magistrates is asking for prejudice.

Most judges are honest, hard-working servants of the public, trying to do the right thing in each case. But, they're also human, and subject to influence. Justices must not only be fair, they must avoid the "appearance of impropriety."

A lawyer who contributes to a judge's election campaign or endorses the candidate should never practice before that judge. It not only appears to be improper, I think it's unethical. This isn't a decision I came to easily. My name appears on literature for some judicial candidates from elections past. In reflection, while writing this book, I concluded that I was wrong to underwrite those candidates if I ever wanted to practice before them. I say this without any qualification. There should never be a case where litigants come before the court with two strikes against them because their counsel missed a patronizing opportunity.

If judges want to be elected, they must do it on records and integrity, not on future paybacks that might be required or at least expected under the current certification policy. Selection of our judges should appear to be as fair as that of big-league umpires.

One final comment about judicial elections—our country has jumped on the bandwagon of term limitations. Someone finally realized that incumbents have a great deal better opportunity to hold their jobs than challengers have of unseating them. Logic tells us why. Incumbents spend tax dollars to send out mailers showing how much they have done for the district. They also vote for programs that make constituents happy. Challengers need to purchase those same stamps and fliers and are unable to enact laws to benefit the people from outside the office.

Judges are in the same position. I know of one judge seeking re-election who collared every attorney who came into court and asked them for sponsorship in chambers. This puts the lawyers in awkward positions. Should they sign an endorsement under such duress? If they don't, future clients could suffer because of an independent act of counsel. The power of the incumbent rests in all branches of government.

It seems reasonable that if we continue in the fiasco of electing judges, then we must limit their terms and forbid attorney endorsements. We don't need career jurists any more than we need a permanent president. The chance of grooming tyrants is too great.

CHAPTER 5

No Soliciting

Lawyers on opposite sides of a case are like the two pairs of shears; they cut what comes between them, but not each other.

Daniel Webster

Some terrorists carry bombs; others tote briefcases. They don't fight with artillery cannons, but with ethical canons, and when those explode, destruction abounds.

Our court system is "protected" from sleazy participants by a set of canons that dissuade lawyers and judges from getting overzealous. The Code of Judicial Conduct controls judges and the Code of Professional Responsibility governs lawyers. Following the canons of those codes shields the legal system and keeps it pure. These guideposts of morality are the pillars that boost public opinion of lawyers above that of used-car salesmen and drug pushers. Without these moral limits, the legal system would be flooded with thieves.

Of course when lawyers interpret any type of rule, they come to whatever result best suits them. So the canons get stretched to the limit by ingenious mental gymnastics.

Most lawyers avoid cases where there is a conflict of interest. If the welfare of one client would be compromised because an attorney represents an adverse client, the attorney refuses the case. Lawyers can't represent one client at the expense of another. An example of the worst case would be if an attorney represented both the plaintiff and the defendant in the same lawsuit. It would be impossible to argue for one side without hurting the other. At least two canons of the Code of Professional Responsibility control this type of behavior.

CANON FIVE

A Lawyer Should Exercise Independent Professional Judgment on Behalf of a Client.

CANON FOUR

A Lawyer Should Preserve the Confidences and Secrets of a Client.

Notice the care taken in wording the rules for ethical conduct. The language guides rather than dictates. If attorneys wanted to avoid all conflicts, it would say "A Lawyer *Shall*" instead of "A Lawyer *Should*." By using the permissive term, attorneys have great latitude in deciding when there is a conflict of interest.

A monumental case blends apparent client conflicts that are but a small nuisance to the attorneys who barbecue everyone in sight on their quest for legal fees. Two huge oil companies, Pennzoil and Texaco, used the same law firm. Pennzoil went through $4 million of legal business a year. Texaco sent the firm another million. When a dispute erupted between the two companies, one would have expected the law firm to opt out of the litigation. Ethical canons seem to dictate it, but instead, Texaco was reportedly asked to waive their objections. The result—Texaco got sued by their own attorneys.

On the surface, this might appear unimportant. But consider that attorneys are privy to the most critical secrets and confidences of their clients. The firm knew, or should have known, many of Texaco's weaknesses by virtue of representing them. Acquiring a waiver from Texaco resolved some problems, but it gets complex. The waiver allowed them to sue their old client, but not to use any confidential information they had regarding Texaco.

Once a secret is known, it can't be unlearned. The lawyers fought with one hand tied behind their backs. They probably knew plenty of soft spots at Texaco that they dared not open, yet they represented Pennzoil against Texaco. An independent attorney who learned of the tender areas would be free to enter an all-out frontal attack. While Pennzoil would never complain about the result they got at trial, it was a precarious tightrope for the firm to walk. When millions of dollars in fees are at stake, the canons stretch.

When the attorneys for Texaco and Pennzoil found themselves with potential conflicts, they danced around the issue until finally justifying their representation. The case was for mega-dollars. In fact, the verdict against Texaco was so huge that it drove the fifth-largest corporation in America into the bankruptcy courts. Lawyers from both sides wanted a piece of that kind of litigation. Conflicts or not, the case went to court, and the lawyers were presumed not to have violated any of the canons.

Mo' Lawyers

Lawyers, like almost everyone else in the country, are driven by greed. This avarice is one of the reasons the country is inundated with lawyers. No one knows exactly how many lawyers there are in this country, but Dan Quayle proclaims that there are 700,000, which he says, is far too many.

All those attorneys and their artillery are necessary, if they're productive, and benefit the people and the economy as a whole. To examine the rewards society gathers by having 700 thousand lawyers, you must venture back to 1776. While Thomas Jefferson penned the Declaration of Independence and John Adams screamed for revolt, a middle-aged Scottish economist produced an astute analysis of capitalism and why it worked.

After Adam Smith wrote *Inquiry into Nature and Causes of the Wealth of Nations*, the free marketplace had its justification. Thinkers like Karl Marx would give the theory a battle, but in the end, capitalism crushed the other political systems.

Smith suggested that greed drove everyone to improve financially. An individual's greed-drive, he said, benefited society because an invisible hand was at work. Industrious individuals produced goods and services in excess, and became wealthy. As individuals pursued riches, they in turn increased the country's total production, which raised the aggregate wealth of the nation. According to the Scottish philosopher, a person's greed isn't only good, it's patriotic.

Smith focused on the big picture. His theory is simplified in the following example: Imagine two wealthy countries ruled by Franklin and Josef. In Franklin's, the industrious people are greedy and work overtime producing goods, while in Josef's, the people are content to be on the government dole and produce nothing. Since both countries are rich, everyone gets all they need, but greed is working its miracle. Josef's people don't work, so the goods they purchase come from Franklin's country. Soon, Franklin's country will have sucked all the money from Josef's land.

What Smith then classified as greed, was really nothing but the well-worn phrase, "work ethic." Smith presumed that people's greed would drive them to ventures that produced something useful that would thereby benefit the nation as a whole. Read on to see how lawyers were able to apply their greed in a way that proved the exception to Smith's theory.

Many attorneys have taken Smith's theories to the extreme by appealing to everyone's greed, including their own. They argue that the more they sue, the better it is for the nation. Our beneficent lawyers commence their patriotic trek to improve the lifestyles of everyone in the nation by swelling their ranks and expanding their workload. In the process, attorneys have made an enemy or two—okay, as a group they're hated by most—but they've also forged some strange partnerships that grant them near impregnable power and wealth.

I touched upon the baseness of some attorneys in the chapter dealing with despicable behavior of judges. Remember that judges are ostensibly the best of the lawyers, so everything said there goes fourfold for the rest of the profession. Newspapers routinely report about sleazy attorneys who steal clients' funds, abuse trust, and blight the world.

For most people, it's difficult to imagine anything positive that lawyers do, but they have their uses. They make excellent thermometers. Any time you see an attorney with his hands in his own pockets, it's really cold.

One Less Lawyer

Steven Spielberg's *Jurassic Park* exhibited some lawyer-bashing of its own by casting the "lawyer" character with several unsavory characteristics. He came across as a wimpy weasel-type who represented the investors in the dinosaur theme park. The developer of the park brought in three scientists who were supposed to convince the lawyer that the reptilian zoo was safe. The scientists, however, were quite negative on the park. The lawyer, disregarding concerns about safety and liability, saw the park as a gold mine.

The developer of the theme park said he couldn't believe that he brought in experts to give approval to the park but the only person supporting it was "a bloodsucking lawyer." It was hard to miss the telegraphing from Spielberg that the legal-beagle would be the movie's first fodder for a pre-historic beast.

Spielberg held a true course as he had the attorney flee from harm's way, stranding two children to face a Tyrannosaurus rex. The chivalrous barrister hid on a toilet in a restroom. Spielberg saved the children by having the king dinosaur blow down the outhouse and pluck the frightened lawyer from the throne.

It's interesting to note that in the novel on which the movie is based, the cowardly character is a publicist!

Paradise Lost

To say many lawyers are greedy is to understate the obvious; to say all other people aren't is a pure canard. Today, the bulk of litigation is greed-driven. This hasn't always been the case. In the decades gone by, many people sued for principle. In turn, their lawyers fought for causes instead of dollars. Civil rights cases were led by *Brown vs. Board of Education,* which began the elimination of segregated schools. Earlier, Japanese citizens sued to be released from FDR's unconscionable internment camps. Later, citizens sued to stop the war in Vietnam. Countless other matters were litigated because wrongs begged for correction.

I don't mean to imply that lawyers don't file cases today on principle, regardless of financial remuneration. Public defenders, prosecuting attorneys, and members of the American Civil Liberties Union (ACLU) are driven primarily by ideals instead of dollars.

Another group that has taken to the courtrooms on principle is the American Center for Law and Justice (ACLJ) headed by Pat Robertson. The ACLJ provides free legal assistance to conservative Christians and reportedly vows to litigate for decades if necessary to restore the nation to its "Godly heritage." It's reported that the group hasn't lost a case in two years.

Now we have an interesting twist going on in the legal community. For years, the ACLU has represented the fringe elements of our society. Their theme has been to protect the Constitution from erosion from all directions. They seem to be color-blind and rest on strong principles, taking on black-activist causes along with those for the Ku Klux Klan.

One of the ACLU goals is to keep God out of the classroom. The *Associated Press* reported that they won a suit to have a portrait of Jesus removed from a high school. The school asked for some modification of the injunction that was won by the ACLU, and was granted a modest reprieve. The court ruled that the portrait is okay to keep hanging if it is completely covered with opaque material. The school's attorney reportedly said: "Like liquor or pornography, a portrait of Jesus must now be wrapped in a plain brown wrapper."

The ACLU opponents in suits like this one could easily be represented by the likes of Pat Robertson's ACLJ. As much as the ACLU wants God out of the classroom, the ACLJ wants Him in. We may be inundated with suits of this kind before the matter is settled.

The problem is that both groups come from the extreme sides of the argument. While Robertson's group claims to vest the right of religion in school to the First Amendment's free-speech clause, the ACLU counters that the same amendment requires a separation of church and state. Both sides will zealously pursue their points of view, and everyone in the middle will get trampled by court rulings that are argued by the fringes of society.

I believe that having a picture of Jesus in a classroom is protected by free speech, which would put me on the side of the ACLJ. However, I also believe that free speech authorizes the Bible and the Koran to be proper educational books for public schools to use. I assume that would line me up against the same group, because they have their own agenda as to who God is and how He should be received in the public schools. However, the ACLU wouldn't join my position because having either religious book available would offend their position to separate church and state. Both groups rest their cases strongly upon the First Amendment.

The reason that the First Amendment is at the beginning of the Bill of Rights is because it is the most important one to maintain our freedoms and liberty. People must be able to say and do what they please if their behavior doesn't injure anyone. Now we will have our most important of amendments narrowed or broadened by lawyers for zealots from the fringes filing suits designed to ram their client's views down the throats of the masses. You have to wonder if the law is ever going to help the people in the middle.

A recent case in Washington State shows how fervently the ACLU goes after principles. Westley Dodd admitted killing two brothers, aged 10 and 11, and a third boy who was 4 years old. These weren't "ordinary" murders, but the sexually deviant kind that turned everyone bitterly against Dodd. After being convicted, and sentenced to die, Mr. Dodd had a choice—he could die by lethal injection or by hanging.

Dodd chose hanging and requested it be done promptly, without any needless appeals. It put his lawyer in a strange position, asking the court to kill his client. In stepped the ACLU, zealously asserting that the state couldn't kill Dodd because hanging was a "cruel and unusual" form of punish-

ment. The ACLU did this on their own. They didn't represent
Dodd, but, like a loose cannon, they fired off a lawsuit to stop
his execution because the method Dodd chose for dying was
barbaric. This was despite Dodd's wishes to be hanged. However, give the ACLU credit, at least the matter was done on
principle instead of for the principal.

Now, consider Rodney King. Every American knows how
brutally the police beat him. An 80-second video of it flooded
the airwaves as the media thrived upon King's thrashing.

Frustration must have culminated when Los Angeles police
finally pulled over the car and got their hands on King. Cops
bludgeoned him to senselessness. Luckily for King, someone
had presence of mind to video-tape the performance instead
of calling out for help. Otherwise, King would have been
another anonymous victim of big brother's nightstick. That
little film made King famous, and potentially rich.

Theoretically, King wants to right the world, to clear the
streets of brutal cops. While correcting the world, he reportedly sold his story for a "substantial" amount according to the
buyer, who is producing a movie.

As time goes on, the value grows. Of course, its value is
being raised by some zealous lawyers who are busy making
the case skyrocket in tort claims. It was reported that three
months after being pummeled, King was afraid to venture out
of his home. His lawyer allegedly hired a psychiatrist to
prescribe antidepressants to King.

Consider what the lawyer has going in this famous mother-
lode of a case. The frightened client remained at home under a
self-imposed house-arrest of sorts. A shrink actively treated
his emotional injuries—depression and fear, not to mention
his obvious physical injuries. This is great for King's civil
case. As a rule, lawyers don't want clients to get better, but
worse. That's because the more paranoid, damaged, and humiliated the client is, the higher the damages go.

His lawyer has a plum. The lawsuit reportedly asked for $83 million. It appears that King wants money. With an incident this notorious, he'll get it. Newspapers reported that King refused a settlement offer of $1.75 million.

Of course, King and the lawyers can argue that the suit is for more than money. It's to make the public aware of police brutality. The theory is that lawsuits will make the police less brutal. But didn't the two criminal trials accomplish that?

In fact, King's civil case does have a higher purpose, and therefore, King has a higher duty. Adam Smith's invisible hand is at work; however, not for the nation as a whole, but for a small and select group. Everyone who filed a case against any police agency for brutality watches King's closely. Mr. King can't accept a pittance for the shellacking he took because he's a major cog in the free-enterprise system.

Settling for too little would lower the worth of all his fellow victims' suits. His case is setting the value for club beatings as surely as Kirby Puckett's signing for $6 million a year set the price for star center-fielders. Far from being a coincidence, another star who plays the same position, Ken Griffey Jr., reportedly signed for the same amount—that's how the free market works. People who took beatings have staked their future wealth on King to get the moon. So have their lawyers. Each of these suits will be paid by taxpayers, and nobody else.

I can't remember a case that got more media coverage than the Rodney King beating trials. A few months after the first trial, despite all the awareness, police in Detroit pulled over a motorist and allegedly bludgeoned him to death with flashlights. The notoriety of Rodney King's case didn't stop the cops in Detroit. Neither did his lawsuit.

We can't let the beatings go unpunished, but on the other hand, those who are beaten shouldn't be made rich. The men and women who died in Desert Storm aren't rewarded for falling to Saddam's henchmen. Why should beatings by cops be worth more than assaults by the little tyrant of the Middle East? Because our legal system says it's right—and it is a fair and honorable one.

Chose The Right Assailant

Justice today depends not only on what happened, but who caused the injury. That is, if money is justice. When a gas company or an airline is potentially liable, attorneys can be the dragon slayers of the world. Should the defendant be an impoverished parolee, lawyers often ignore the plight of the victim.

The reason is a creative mechanism lawyers invented called the *contingency fee*. When an attorney takes on a case, the payment for services is usually on a per hour basis, a flat fee, or a contingency fee. A person might hire a lawyer on an hourly basis to close a real-estate transaction. Some lawyers prepare simple wills for a flat fee of $200, regardless of the time it takes them to do the work. Finally, there is the fee that is contingent upon the award won by the attorney for the client.

Most cases involving personal injuries are handled on a contingency. If the client wins, then a percentage of the award is used for lawyer fees. In a personal-injury suit, the fees are as much as 50 percent of the money that is collected. It's through the use of these fees that impoverished people can purchase the tickets to the lottery. But the attorney must be skilled in screening out these cases. Only the ones that will net a sizable fee are considered. Many people have valid claims that go unattended because they can't afford to hire a lawyer or the suit won't generate enough money for an attorney to take a chance on a contingency.

Calling All Victims

Some lawyers live off suing. Unfortunately, they can run out of work and starve. Fear not, because they are also an enterprising lot, and they can generate demand for their services out of thin air. They are always looking for new targets and new sources of clients. That's one reason they began suing doctors so vociferously; they needed to expand the archery range and line up a new set of targets.

Besides targets, lawyers also need and rely on a huge supply of clients. A great vehicle for finding lawsuits is to chase ambulances. Some unscrupulous attorneys drive around with scanners going in their cars so they can locate the bad traffic accidents and pass about their business cards. Many survive by that practice alone.

Injury accidents and medical malpractice are sought-after cases because they generate huge fees. A lawyer who writes wills and fights out custody battles or defends people from the hangman's noose earns a pittance compared to the personal-injury lawyer. Like a commissioned salesman, it's where the megabucks are in law.

The lawyer then gambles on winning. It takes years for most non-tort attorneys to earn what a single million-dollar suit nets a plaintiff's lawyer. These suits are lawyers' opium. The lure of them is irresistible—and winning one is addictive. When the greed bug hits, it's public beware because lawyers are too smart to inject poison into their own veins—they dig into everyone else's. To discover how enamored attorneys are by contingency-fee cases, consider lawyer advertisements. Any number of them boldly proclaim, "No Attorney Fees Unless We Win," or similar language.

There was a time when advertising was too undignified to soil the legal profession. However, in trying to bring the profession into the twentieth century and assure their brethren plenty of work, the Supreme Court opened the floodgates for wholesale pursuit of clients and created plenty of legal work by allowing the predators new snares. The Court said lawyers had the right to advertise for new clients. The logic of the decision rests solidly in the First Amendment, or free speech. The Court decided that advertising for lawsuits was protected speech. Before this ruling, lawyers were forced to seek clients by word-of-mouth. Now, lawyer advertisements are prevalent. Attorneys electronically vie for lucrative *wrongful-death, personal-injury,* and *automobile-accident* cases. Some lawyers even boast at how much they "won" for certain clients in their advertisements.

The worst of the lot are on television depicting slimy-looking insurance adjusters cajoling unsuspecting victims into signing releases of liability while in the hospital. It takes great creativity to convince the audience in a 30-second commercial that insurance adjusters are sleazier than lawyers.

The message couldn't be clearer: *Come to us and we'll get you lots of money.* Lawyers play on the greed of prospective clients to get new cases. Adam Smith's theory appears to be at work again. Lawyer greed should benefit the whole society.

Unfortunately, the equation is distorted. Most litigation sucks resources from the world. Lawsuits usually do nothing but make people miserable. The process haunts plaintiffs and defendants alike until the parties become obsessed with the case. It drives at their sanity and makes them all less productive.

Luckily, lawyers aren't bothered by such mundane emotions, as their file cabinets full of misery prove. For every file in the barrister's drawer that tags a lawsuit, there are at least two parties suffering during the entire process. Since most cases take several months or years to conclude, each suit represents an enormous amount of lost productivity. Adam

Smith was brilliant, but he hadn't considered anything close to our bloated legal system.

Tasteless ads will continue, often in the yellow pages of telephone books. And with the Rodney King verdict in Los Angeles, look for huge banners for lawyers seeking victims of "Police Brutality." "Breast Implant" recipients will also be targeted by attorneys since the silicone scare has been brought to the front page of many newspapers. However, the award for the most atrocious ad that I have seen in any yellow pages, goes to Larry H. Parker, of Long Beach, California. In the 1991 telephone book he took out a full-page ad that showed photographs of four of his clients with a settlement amount beside each of them—displayed like a hunter's trophy animals. In screaming 5/8" block letters is the grand prize as the ad blazes:

"LARRY PARKER GOT ME $2.1 MILLION"

This shows how much lawyers want to grab the big cases. To do this they play on the "greed need" of the public. Protected by the First Amendment and free speech, Larry Parker promotes litigation by means of such advertisement.

A friend of mine, a good attorney who competently runs his practice, saw me researching wrongful-death cases in the law library one morning. He asked, "Do you have a good one?" I said that I was researching a book and not a case of my own. He said, "Wouldn't you know it? For ten years I practiced without a wrongful-death case. Then, this last year, two come into my office. But, both were traffic accidents and the parties at fault were uninsured. There's no way to tie liability to a deep-pocket, so the cases will net me nothing."

That explains how lawyers long for personal-injury suits, and wrongful-death cases are among the best money-makers. It also shows that our system is violently flawed. If you are killed by a pauper, your family gets nothing. If you get killed by an agent of a deep-pocketed company, your family gets millions. Likewise, being raped by Mike Tyson could mean lots of money, while a rape by an unknown masher will usually net you zero. In either case, you are just as dead or just as violated. Having a good case isn't enough, it must also be against someone who has money. Most torts go unrewarded because the responsible party is broke. The critical key to our judicial lottery is that you must be bloodied by a wealthy party. Justice boils down to money. Our tort system runs and thrives upon it. It's being swallowed by gluttonous lawyers and litigants alike as they gamble with our own decency.

Pop Go The Weasels

When food poisoning struck the Northwest, lawyers took advantage of the opportunity and the news media went into overdrive as both stuffed themselves on miserable victims.

The suspected cause of the outbreak was a local fast-food hamburger chain, Jack-in-the-Box. The restaurants had allegedly served hamburgers loaded with E. coli 0157:H7, which is a polite way of saying too much of the meat came from the rectum, and too little from the flanks.

E. coli is a bacteria that usually dies when cooked, but when it survives, it can be deadly. Consumption of tainted food reportedly sickened at least 500 people in western Washington state. About 92 percent of those cases allegedly came from eating undercooked hamburgers at Jack-in-the-Box restaurants.

Youngsters took the brunt of the onslaught as the maleficent bacteria killed at least three children and hospitalized more than 125 who survived. Many victims suffered kidney failure and received dialysis treatments.

When the problem occurred, the company responded almost immediately. The firm's president, Robert Nugent, reportedly offered to pay medical expenses, "immediately, with no strings attached." The position of the corporation was that it would attempt to do what was morally right from the onset of the epidemic. Bear in mind that this was caused by a tragic accident. No malice is attributed in any way.

Long after the illnesses run their malignant courses, Foodmaker, Inc., the parent company of Jack-in-the-Box, will pay the price. Payment started when the newspapers printed macabre articles focusing on the stricken children. Blame-laden broadcasts also filled radio and television sets with traumatic tales about the victims of E. coli. Bad publicity fueled public concern of the crippled business. Sales were off by as much as 35 percent.

An enterprising lawyer took hold of the opportunity by running a quarter-page ad in both Seattle newspapers that targeted bacterial victims. The lawyer was attacked by the Washington State Trial Lawyers Association for "opportunistic advertising" that "does a great disservice to injury victims and our profession." The following is a portion of the ad:

IMPORTANT NOTICE

If you or someone you know has been
stricken by the recent outbreak of

E Coli 0157 : H7 Bacterium
DUE TO UNDERCOOKED HAMBURGER

you may have a valuable legal claim for
DAMAGES

The attorney responded to the criticism in two ways. First, he said that he didn't set up shop at the Dallas airport after a crash like other lawyers did.

Second, he claimed to be interested in helping people. He added that he received harassing telephone calls from citizens who didn't understand how committed he is to rectifying an egregious wrong in the beef industry.

The media got into the act, carrying prominent articles about the lawyer, giving him far more publicity than his paid-for advertisements could have ever accomplished. To augment this, television and radio filled the air with the story. Media bombardment and suits from attorneys are inevitable in any catastrophic outbreak. These will drag on, padding the billfolds of lawyers, and selling many newspapers.

Retired Chief Justice Warren E. Burger recently expressed his views about lawyer ads. Burger declared that "huckster advertising" by lawyers has taken the profession to "its lowest ebb in the history of our country." Adding some emphasis to the characterization of lawyers who advertise, Burger said:

> Perhaps "huckster" is not strong enough a word; "shyster" is more appropriate but... even "shyster" is not strong enough.

A few victims will strike gold and win millions as their parents file into court to reap the rewards of a system bent upon unequal application of justice. Had the contaminated beef been served at a struggling diner, there would be no awards for those injured because there would be no money to pay them. The "civic-minded" lawyer would probably have neglected to advertise for victims, and other attorneys would stand in line to avoid cases with no chance of money. However, since Jack-in-the-Box has deep pockets, there's cash aplenty to feed the sharks.

Many will applaud the righteous lawyers who litigate for justice of the afflicted as litigation floodgates burst. Attorneys will grab this attention since they get precious-little positive press. But, consider that the dragon the counselors are after has reportedly admitted a tragic mistake and offered to cover medical expenses. Further, the stores announced specific programs in food preparation which will greatly reduce the chances of any similar recurrence. So, what will the suits prove?

In a free-enterprise economy, it's the consumer who makes or breaks all businesses. If the public concludes that the restaurants are indeed safe and forgives them for the tragic accident, Jack-in-the-Box will flourish. Should patrons avoid the stores, the chain is doomed.

People should treat this catastrophe for what it is—a terrible accident—and view with great skepticism anyone who profits from unfortunate children who paid with their bodies and souls.

The Defense Budget

Lawyer greed has impacted the medical profession. The cost of medical care is rising beyond the reach of many Americans as our elected representatives chase health-care reform. To understand how the price of medicine skyrocketed, lawyers and their greedy courtroom partners must be discussed.

When Bush and Clinton battled for chief executive, the vice-presidential candidates debated. In that forum, Quayle said that the multitude of attorneys and their lawsuits bash citizens with $23 billion every year for *defensive medicine*. His boss, not to be outshone by an understudy, took the estimate further by claiming the number was *$25* billion.

Of course, paying an astronomical amount is acceptable if it serves a good purpose, and defensive medicine sounds protective and positive. In medicine, like in sports, a good defense prevents opponents from scoring. Super Bowl teams have stellar defenses. Super doctors are just as defensive as their sporting counterparts.

The question to answer is: Who lines up opposite the doctors? While first thoughts point to vile diseases and heinous injuries, cheers rise for the physicians. However, rudimentary screening of the problem shows the defensive medicine isn't necessarily used to heal the afflicted. A vast majority of it is needless medicine used for protection from lawyers while being thrust directly against the best interests of patients. Some sources offer that perhaps 25 percent of all medical costs are needless.

Even the New England Journal of Medicine reports that defensive medicine is practiced increasingly by doctors to guard against lawsuits. In the process, the physicians order superfluous tests and overuse preventive measures. Doctors, the article explains, avoid treating some diseases because of the legal liability. One in eight obstetricians stopped delivering babies because of it. Then the article—written primarily for physicians—says that the liability problems affect doctor-patient relationships adversely and *may* increase the cost of care.

There was a time when medical ethics dictated that illness or injury be present before treatment was undertaken. However, physicians need to earn a living and they're an enterprising lot. To boost the need for care beyond when illness or injury is absent, they promote with the idea of wellness checks. They sell the concept to the public as annual physicals, paps, and general checkups.

As a by-product of the doctor's desire to sell more services, the medical community developed the idea of *preventive medi-*

cine. It confirms Smith's belief of the invisible-hand theory. The doctor's "greed" drove them to seek wealth. In the process, this greed brought about a healthier, longer-living, and more productive work force.

Smith's theory works fine in preventive medicine. Doctors sought more fees, but were benefiting everyone by keeping their patients healthier. By employing the procedures, they're able to stop some cancers before it's too late, and the early checks often allow treatment and cure of otherwise debilitating diseases. Wellness checks probably extend the lives of many patients. They make sense; they help the patients despite lining the pockets of the health-care providers simultaneously.

While doctors have a vested interest in confusing the public with the two terms, people must separate benefits from *preventive medicine* with the horrors of *defensive medicine*. As great as some preventive medicine is, its defensive counterpart is disgusting. Adam Smith's principle of greed benefiting the population at large fails in defensive medicine because it's anti-productive.

While it makes sense to spend several dollars on polio vaccinations for your child and purchase viable protection, should you also spend thousands on CT and MRI scans every time the youngster has a headache? Many of those procedures are ordered on the rare chance that the patient could have some serious ailment that will show up on the test. Doctors don't want to let the rare one through—or they might get sued—so they subject many patients to the needless tests. If the patient is without means to pay for the testing, then the welfare system pays it and the taxpayers get stuck.

Physicians, who have a great deal of interest in avoiding liability for malpractice, love these scans along with most other lab work. There's little chance of being sued for ordering a test, and a great risk in refusing to do so. In addition, some doctors who order the tests might receive a payment and many also have direct interests in the labs that do the testing.

Doctors blame the lawyers for defensive medicine. Physicians claim that when suits stop, everyone will profit by cheaper, higher quality health care. Well, as huge as $25 billion is, it pales when compared to useless medicine that Americans endure that is totally unrelated to *either* preventive or defensive medicine. *Consumer Reports* estimated five times that amount is spent annually on clearly unnecessary procedures.

While the discussion so far has dealt with how the "greed" of the doctors and lawyers injures the patient financially, it hasn't touched upon the emotional trauma. Imagine the pain that parents feel while watching their children get strapped in for a "cat scan" that scares the youngsters more than a Stephen King novel. Being subjected to these dreadful tests could cause psychological damage to the little ones.

Then consider the anxiety felt while awaiting the results, and how that wears on the patients, and especially parents of youngsters who are shuffled through the wasted tests. And, finally, even after the results give a clean bill of health, there is the constant gnawing in the back of one's mind that there must have been something amiss, or the drastic test wouldn't have been ordered by a doctor. It's a total screw job.

Should the blame go to the doctor? I believe not, at least not for all of it. The real culprit is our society. In our greedy pedestrian ways, we try to gouge everyone for every cent that's available. It's the American way.

Of course, doctors aren't the only ones who suffer from our litigation mills. Lawyers sue airlines, auto manufacturers, cities, teachers, and anyone with a buck that can be grabbed. Similarly, countermeasures like defensive medicine aren't limited to the medical profession. It's prevalent everywhere. Butchers, bakers, and barristers practice it. A cost is added to everything that's done to cover the potential litigation expense.

One of the most critical places it occurs is in the workplace. Employers who have any acumen screen every prospective employee as a potential litigant. Personnel managers may deny it, but if they hear any discussion remotely touching on lawsuits or accident claims in an interview, the candidate is out of luck. The reason is that once someone has sued, it's that much easier for them to sue again. The process is addictive. Employers don't like to go to court to defend how they run their companies.

Many "disgruntled" employees make a killing suing for sexual harassment, wrongful discharge, discrimination, or other "abuses" in the workplace. This doesn't mean that these behaviors should be condoned, but consider their impact. As surely as the $25 billion of defensive medicine costs the consumer, so does every one of these lawsuits against employers.

Businesses keep records solely for justifying a possible termination of an employee. The person who snoops and organizes the files costs money, which is all passed on to the consumer, but it's far worse than that. Just as the trust is lost in the doctor-patient relationship because of defensive medicine, so is it lost at the workplace. Managers are constantly looking for bad behavior to justify a firing that might happen years hence. Employees know this is going on, so they're constantly looking over their shoulders for the boogyman. I'd call it paranoia, except the fear of having someone give you demerits in any workplace is a very real one.

Dutch Treat

Lawyers' greed has few limits as it preys on tragedy. I can only think of one industry that needs misery and suffering as much as lawyers—the media. Television cameras are often on the scene of disasters before the police and rescue units arrive. They thrive on disaster.

When a Boeing *El Al* cargo jet crashed into an apartment house near Amsterdam, it was feared that more than 200 people died in the wreck. Agents for *Reuters, AP, CNN,* and the major networks flocked to get sensational stories of human suffering. Pictures hit televisions and newspapers alike.

Our breed of trial lawyers weren't to be outdone by those media-types. Within a week of the crash, American attorneys swooped into Holland, picking through the debris like vultures at a kill site. An American attorney held a news conference in the Netherlands to "communicate to the citizens of Holland what their rights are in America." You see, many of those Dutchmen were ignorant of our personal-injury tort system.

What our lawyers don't understand, or choose to ignore, is something basic to Dutch tradition. They aren't yet driven by the American get-rich-off-misery scheme. In the Netherlands there is almost no precedent for suits for damages. Moreover, Dutch lawyers are forbidden from taking cases on contingency of winning.

The scavengers' invasion so offended the Dutch people that residents were warned by the press and the bar association to shun the greedy American lawyers. It's a given that the Dutch courts won't be quick to let those American attorneys file suits in the Netherlands, but if lawyers from the U.S. can get clients from Holland, then they can file a suit in America.

One enterprising American lawyer was reported as saying: "We're not trying to intrude upon Dutch practitioners. We're trying to assist them." Yeah, with our help, the Dutch can enjoy such niceties as defensive medicine.

Wait A Bleating Moment

A telling example of how repulsive lawsuits are for medical well-being appeared in a newspaper article that quoted a doctor from the Mayo Clinic who called the price of a drug "inexcusable." The drug in question is *levamisole* and is used in the treatment of colorectal cancer. An expansive study showed how effective the drug was in treatment. The doctor claimed that the yearly cost for treating a cancer patient with the drug is $1,495, and that, he reportedly said, was an egregious overcharge.

To back up his argument, the doctor explained that the drug is no new kid on the block, but has been around for 30 years. Treating colon cancer is just a new use that was found for it. Further, the cost of research and development for it was paid by the government.

The maker of the drug responded that "it is fairly and reasonably priced for a life-saving drug." Lest the good doctor be taken for a bleating fool, one more portion of his averment is critical. The medicine is also used to worm animals. The same annual supply for a human that costs almost $1,500 can be purchased for sheep at $14 per annum. It costs 100 times as much to buy levamisole for people.

It's commonplace for poor people to eat dog food because that's all they can afford. Now, they'll use their pet's suppositories, too. And it isn't too difficult to guess why there is such a discrepancy in cost—*sheep don't sue.*

CHAPTER 6

Inside The Sue-er

Nothing can be solved in the crisis in our courts without first getting inside the minds of the people who play the game of suing. In civil cases, it is the plaintiffs who start all lawsuits. It is not the lawyers, as is popularly believed. Think about it. How can a lawyer start a lawsuit without a client?

As discussed earlier, lawyers are creative in locating clients who don't know they need a lawsuit. However, many cases are born in the minds of the wannabe litigants.

There are many reasons why people sue. Unfortunately, too many lawyers don't care why; their only concern is what's in it for them. Here's a list of the more prevalent reasons why people start lawsuits:

For Money: One of the first things that comes to anyone's mind when discussing lawsuits is money. People often sue to get it.

I recall a story about a guy who tried to hire a lawyer. He explained how he slipped and fell on a water-soaked floor in a supermarket. When the lawyer asked if he went to the doctor, he replied, "No." When asked if he had missed any work, he replied, "No." When asked if he had been injured, he replied, "No." Finally, he was asked why he was in a lawyer's office, and he replied, "To see what it's worth." He was told the lottery office was just down the street.

For Justice: Some litigants have no interest in financial awards. Their only desire is to right a wrong. They want the wrongdoer to admit the mistake and receive a reasonable punishment.

As an example, if a woman were maimed by an incompetent doctor she might want to challenge the quack's right to practice medicine. The suit might not be for money damages. But, even if the jury awarded money, it would probably go to charity. All this person wants is to make sure the doctor doesn't get away with it.

For Principle: "For justice" and "for principal" are nearly interchangeable. To draw the main distinction between them, consider that people who are out for the principle of the matter generally are altruistic. A principle suit is usually brought for the sake of others, as opposed to benefiting just the plaintiff.

When Rosa Parks refused to give up her seat and go to the back of the bus, she started a suit based on the principle that segregation was wrong. She didn't want money, she just wanted some respect.

For Revenge: People out for revenge simply want to get even. They're the type who might punch your lights out, or take the more respectable route of dragging your assets into court. These people want nothing but a payback. They will build a "spite" fence 10 feet high solely to block a neighbor's view of the lake.

A man who was divorcing his wife asked an attorney to represent him. During the conference, he said that he wanted the family dog. Upon learning that the spouse would fight for the dog, the attorney told her client that the retainer would go up $3,000 if they were going into a custody fight over a puppy. At that point, the client said to forget the canine. Obviously, he didn't want the dog, but he knew how much his wife loved it.

For Authority: We all know people who are power hungry. And, for the most part, we try to stay out of their way. They want to teach others not to cross them. Anyone who does will feel their wrath.

Case in point: A child's parents were angered that their son had been slapped around by his teacher. While they didn't mind the local gang members beating him up, they were damned if they would allow a teacher to. They sued to show their son that they had power over his teacher—who had power over their son. It was nothing more than a case of pulling rank and putting the teacher in his place.

For Conflict: Surprisingly, some people thrive on conflict. They live for the sake of agitating others. It was for these people that the word "harass" was invented. They aren't interested in talking out any problems; they want war. Another example of people to stay away from.

A friend of mine represented a fellow who brought him a new lawsuit so often it seemed like every month. My buddy gave this troublemaker the heave-ho when he finally realized his client wanted to stir hornet nests wherever he went. This guy ended too many conversations with, "You'll hear from my lawyer."

For The Thrill: Like the high-rolling gambler who isn't excited unless he has a huge bet on the table, this guy is driven by adrenalin rushes. He goes to court like he goes to the casino—for broke. This guy would never negotiate—he's an all-or-nothing player. Even lawyers try to stay clear of people like this.

For Attention: Andy Warhol said that everyone gets their 15 minutes of fame. Unfortunately, for all too many, that 15 minutes comes in the courtroom.

A forgotten movie star or an up-and-coming actor falls squarely into the category of an attention-seeking litigant. Newspapers are full of stories about aging stars who seek attention in the courts by filing frivolous suits.

The Rest Of The Combatants

There are several other reasons that people sue and they probably should be addressed. Some think of zealots as a group by themselves. These people are so inflexible, so obsessed, and so unreasonable that they represent the extreme fringe of the group who fight "for principle."

Another group so badly misunderstands a particular situation that they force a trial. These people can misperceive due to mental illness, stubbornness, or ignorance. Their failed perception puts them into the fringe of the "for justice" group.

Some people don't want to be in court at all, but they were forced into starting the action. They didn't instigate the suit. These people don't fall into any particular group; they might be in court because their neighbor erected a "spite" fence.

And, In This Corner

Defendants are the people who get sued by the plaintiffs. Defendants fight courtroom battles against those who have challenged them to a duel. Like with plaintiffs, there are several reasons that enter into a person's decision to defend. Some are valid, and others are as bogus as the reasons to sue.

If they are "just plain folks," defendants have one advantage going into court: Americans root for underdogs and many defendants are seen as such. The country fell in love with the 1969 "Miracle Mets" because the team was so inept in prior years. When odds get piled against someone, Americans might rally around him. That is why some defendants in lawsuits get public support, even though they often deserve none. Following are some reasons people defend themselves in lawsuits:

For Necessity: This is the flip-side of a "for money" plaintiff. These people are down on their luck and out of cash. They are well-intended and want to pay their debts, but they're broke. When settlement talks fail, or their creditors lose patience, these people are brought to court.

A woman who lost her job after ten years couldn't pay the bills. Her bank ran out of patience, and started foreclosure proceedings on her home. The woman fought the action, knowing she was delinquent, but wanting to keep her home. She hoped to find another job, save her home, and pay her debts. By fighting the matter in court, she stalled the foreclosure and bought enough time to do just that.

For Justice: Much like the counter-part plaintiff, these defendants go to court because it would be unjust not to do so. "For justice" defendants probably don't want to be in court, but feel they must be.

A boy dashed out of nowhere, into the path of a man's car. The man swerved, but still hit the boy. When the unartful dodger sued, the driver felt it would be wrong not to fight. He didn't think that he could have avoided the accident.

For Principle: The distinction between "for principle" plaintiffs and defendants is that a plaintiff usually wants to change something, while a defendant wants to maintain the status quo.

An elementary school put on Christmas programs for decades with traditional songs and decorations. When they were sued to take Jesus out of Christmas, they defended.

For Weaseling: These litigants must be brought to court. They don't honor obligations and slither from responsibility. Everyone has run into these people. They promise everything, and produce nothing. When frustrated people finally recognize they're dealing with weasels and file suit, these defendants are adept at finding "weasel" attorneys to represent them.

A weasel answered a classified ad and purchased a car from an unsuspecting private party. The payment was with a check that the weasel post-dated without telling the seller. Upon presenting the check to her bank, the seller learned that she must wait 7 days before the check could be cashed. Before the week was up, the weasel closed the bank account, leaving the sucker with a worthless piece of paper.

For Obstinacy: These people are stubborn and while they know they're wrong, they defend by saying: "Show me." Obstinate defendants force plaintiffs to jump over every procedural hurdle, hoping they can't prove their case. Most criminal defense work is done obstinately.

Knowing they were infringing on a small competitor, a huge corporate defendant fought a lawsuit to finality. The corporation hoped to exhaust their insignificant opponent to the point where "the little guy" ran out of money. The jury saw through the gambit and smartly spanked the obstinate behemoth.

For Intimidation: Intimidators come from both sides of the lawsuit, but frequently are the defendants. They live by the adage that "the best defense is a good offense." These defendants frequently press phony counter-claims in court to divert attention from the real issues.

A grocery store attempted to collect its bill from a customer who refused to pay. When a suit started, the customer claimed that the store discriminated against him because he was black. The counter-claim was totally frivolous, but the store dropped their complaint, figuring it was better to lose $200 than to face exposure for a civil-rights violation.

Mix And Match

As with plaintiff categories, defendant mind-sets blend together. Not every litigant fits into a pigeon hole. And each category can cross from plaintiff to defendant. Sadists should be disdained, but instead are glorified by courts. These people enjoy beating others, and our system actually encourages them. Sadists want to make life miserable for others and can be plaintiffs or defendants. A mix of "for authority," "for obstinacy," and "for weaseling" gives them a full-fledged character-disorder.

At the other end of the spectrum are the masochists, who like to be slapped around. When they get a chance to go a courting, they squirm with delight as the plaintiff wails away. These people mix "for conflict," "for the thrill," and "for attention" together and enjoy judicial abuse.

Keeping The Court At Bay

It's been discussed that lawsuits make people miserable. Except for those litigants suffering from character disorders, almost everyone would rather be anywhere than court. It's stressful for the parties, the witnesses, and the lawyers. For those, and other reasons, the vast majority of cases settle out of court.

The heart of why people sue is because there is a conflict. Each civil case revolves around a dispute that requires resolution. When parties want a trial, the matter goes to court. Bear in mind that almost every trial is brought to court because reason can't be used to settle the matter.

Were reason in the offing, the parties would have probably settled the matter themselves. Or they might have hired a lawyer to "reason" the right attitude into their opponent. When lawyers can't settle a dispute, they reach into a bag of tricks. Contrary to popular belief, lawyers don't like trials. It's more profitable and certain to settle cases out of court. To avoid trials, lawyers often use a process called *mediation*.

Mediation is a procedure where the parties are brought together to discuss the conflict by presenting their stories to a mediator who listens and attempts to guide them into a reasonable settlement. A mediator has no power to force a solution and only offers advice.

Mediation is informal, expedient, and relatively inexpensive. It has the advantage of ending a matter quickly and quietly. For most litigants, it is a desirable and appealing alternative to going to trial. Mediation can even take place before a suit is filed, saving court time and public humiliation. Since the process is informal (hence, not laden with procedural traps for the unwary), many parties can adequately represent themselves without lawyers.

With all that going for it, why don't all cases get solved in mediation? Because, some litigants don't want them to. Either they're jealous of another, or they want to spite them, or they believe it would be unjust to let another off without a trial. Sometimes they mistake a weak case for a strong one, making a compromise improbable. But, many times it's pure unreasonableness on the part of one or both parties.

Consider a heated divorce where the couple held a season ticket for a professional sports team. When the club made it into the playoffs, the parties fought over who got to go to the games. Their lawyers couldn't settle it. The warring spouses actually took up court time with it, forcing a judge to decide who would watch the games. Litigants with mind-sets like this soon-to-be ex-husband and ex-wife couldn't talk reason about anything; their emotions clouded the issues. When people are that vindictive, hateful, or ridiculous, they need trials. Mediation requires participation, reduces conflict, and settles disputes. However, it can't work when divorce proceedings are filled with venom.

When a lawyer can't settle a case through mediation, they reach back into their bag and pull out a stronger amulet. This one is called *arbitration*, which is a bit like mediation, except the arbitrator has the power to order a resolution. After hearing the merits of the case, the arbitrator makes a ruling, which resolves the dispute... unless one or both of the parties are so dissatisfied with the result that they take the matter to a "real" court.

One reason parties shy away from arbitrators is because the process is viewed by many as a "kangaroo" court. Besides the perception of arbitration being a "toy court," it has an additional prong that bites at lawyers and litigants alike. If a party allows an arbitrator to hear the matter and the party decides to go to court afterward, there is a possibility of punishment. When an arbitrator's award is higher than a party receives in court, there is often a penalty the party must pay.

How are we going to convince people that arbitration is a viable alternative when they see it as a pseudo court, made worse because they might even be penalized for trying arbitration in the first place?

Torts And Tarts

Many big-dollar cases are for torts. Before I entered law school, I thought torts were pastries. While in school, I learned that they were civil wrongs, things that can be righted by lawsuits. After completing my degree and watching some jury verdicts soar beyond the stratosphere, I think of torts as crimes. Unfortunately, the criminals are also the victims—the American people.

It is a tort to cause damage to someone or something because of negligent, reckless, or intentional action other than in a contractual breach. Lawyers love to use terms like this. They mystify the law. Obscurity is the main tool. The less understandable the terms, the more needed are attorneys. Many people are uncertain whether a negligent act is worse than a reckless one.

An example may help. While driving his car, if Jerry brakes too late and rear ends a truck at a traffic light, Jerry is negligent. He misjudged the stopping distance and caused the accident. If he knows his brakes are bad and about to fail, but continues driving the car, risking an accident, his degree of liability increases. If he rear ends the same truck now, he is reckless. Finally, if Jerry is mad and hits the truck for spite, he acted intentionally.

The level of liability rating is:

Negligent is bad. Someone failed to use due care and caution and caused an injury. Harm from negligence is usually called an accident.

Reckless is much worse. Someone knew or should have known their actions were dangerous.

Intentional is the worst level of tort. Someone decided they wanted to break something and did it.

The Greening Of America

Things turn around for fair play and wrongs are corrected. So goes the theory of our law of torts. Attorneys believe that when someone is damaged, an award of money will compensate them for the injury. Money is the root of all remedies. And why not? We live in a society driven by green.

Where can you get stung by a bee and win more than a million dollars? Where can you try for a million when poked by a needle? In court, that's where. America's rabid tort system is not only frothing, it's gasping.

Who can we blame for such ridiculous results? The lawyers? They're always a good target. Not much love for them. Even the bard declared that we should kill them all. And in this matter they have a great deal of responsibility.

Who else? The politicians? Another fine target. They fit the description of corrupt and greedy quite nicely.

The lottery? It seems that these get-rich-for-a-buck schemes have affected us to further greed.

How about us? We, the people, in order to form a more perfect pocket book, and live on someone else's money, do hereby declare that lotteries can be had by drawings of chance or in courts of law.

A Terrific Tort

Many cases begin like this one: In a small apartment an infant awaited her bath. At 9 months of age, she easily fit into the bathroom sink. Her mother checked the water for proper temperature as the baby splashed. Having lived in the same dwelling for one and one-half years, mom felt comfortable with the surroundings. She knew her way around the place and reacted quickly when trouble erupted.

In the living room, a 2-year-old boy crashed into a table and hit his head. Mom rushed to comfort the fallen boy, leaving baby in the bathroom sink. Up stepped baby's 3-year-old brother to help. He turned on the hot water faucet and waited. Scalding water flowed from the tap, measured at 143 degrees Fahrenheit, searing baby's torso as it cooked her tiny legs. So painful was the water as it boiled over her skin that the infant cried, but nothing came from her tiny mouth except a high-pitched peep. The brother who turned on the water went into the living room and understated the situation, "Baby needs help."

Four years of excellent medical care and $340,000 later, the child is most of what she could have been. Still, she remains scarred from the waist down, with irreparable injuries by current medical standards.

Mom hired an attorney and sued the manufacturers of the hot water heater, the makers of the thermostat, the building's owners, a plumbing company, and the gas company.

Several theories supported the suit. The manufacturer of the water heater allegedly installed a dangerous thermostat. It was marked "warm" for its coolest setting and "hot" for the highest temperature. A raised dash in the middle of the setting appeared to be the normal setting. That is exactly where the heater was set when it spewed out 143 degrees of scalding fury. One would have reasonably expected a heater to be set in the moderate range to be a moderate temperature, but it wasn't the case.

The owners of the apartment ended up in court for allegedly providing unsafe living quarters, with the water temperature set dangerously high. The owners hired plumbers for annual inspections required by law. Those plumbers were said to be negligent in allowing such a ferocious setting and wound up in court.

The gas company lined up with the rest of the defendants for supplying the fuel that cooked the water. And finally, there reportedly weren't any warning labels declaring that water at 143 degrees scalds even adults.

Bringing in several defendants is a common legal tactic. The logic behind this move is that the more defendants there are, the more money there is available in the case. Anyone who listens to Bruce Williams, a consumer advocate who is heard on national radio, has learned that, "You sue everyone in sight." Plaintiffs are quick to name as many defendants as possible. Strategically, the move makes great sense. If you bring in the wrong parties, they can move for a dismissal and walk away from the court. This type of reasoning is unconscionable. It wrongly presumes that being sued and later having the case dismissed is a minor inconvenience to the defendant. However, should a plaintiff forget a person, the suit might be doomed to a successful verdict without a chance of collecting any award. This isn't a minor flaw in the system, it's a tragic one.

Baby's attorney confirmed that the burns received by the young girl were horrible. Medical and therapy expenses of $400,000 are expected in the future. This was a catastrophic injury. Had there not been a suit and a settlement, someone would have absorbed a huge medical bill. The legal system in this case churned out a settlement of $15 million.

Terrible as it is to have an infant horribly burned, one can't but consider the result. Fifteen million dollars is such a staggering figure that most people can't even comprehend it. If the girl spent $1,000 a day it would take 41 years to consume the award. That is, if the money is in a mattress and earning absolutely no interest. How can a 4-year-old girl spend $1,000 a day? She will probably have to pay for her medical and therapeutic expenses from the past and the future. Together, that will amount to about $750 thousand. She'll likewise have to pay her lawyer a huge fee. If the contingency is the standard one-third, it will be $5 million. But, if her mother continues to take care of her until she is 18 years old, she won't need to spend any money until then. Investing the remaining $9 million at a modest 5 percent per year after-tax growth would net her almost $18 million on her 18th birthday.

The lure of an award such as this will catch many a fish. In 1990 the average American worker earned $23,602. Pick 381 average wage earners off the street and ask them to give you their earnings for the year. If they all cooperate, you will also have $9 million.

But people forget the heinous burns, and see only the dollars. In my private practice I've had many prospective clients relate tales of injury only to finish with the line, "What's it worth?" Sadly, they have read the newspaper accounts of huge awards and want in on the action.

The House That Jack Built

Consider the liability of the parties with this morose verse.

The gas works pumped the fuel
that boiled the water
in the bad tank
that ran too hot
from thermostatic fault
that plumbers missed
that bubbled the kettle
that burned the baby
that lay in the sink
in the house that Jack built.

While the use of a nursery rhyme is callous considering the horrific burns the little girl received, it shows the directional heading of our courts. Our legal system bases fault upon the logic of "The House that Jack Built." Everyone remembers from their childhood about the famous cow with the crumpled horn that tossed the dog, that worried the cat, that killed the rat, that ate the malt, that lay in the house that Jack built.

Coincidentally, esteemed jurists use the contrived reasoning of the old verse. If Jack kept a tidy house, the cow wouldn't have tossed the dog because it wouldn't have scared the cat and so on down to the malt left out for the rat. The rhyme holds every actor responsible. The cause sequence in the burned child's case is as foolish as "The House that Jack Built" except for one thing. It isn't a rhyme anymore. It's the law.

Guilt clung to everyone, like musty clothes from a mildewed chest. The causal chain bound the defendants until they settled. It was a compromise borne out of fear about what an impassioned jury might render under the tragic circumstances. The plumber, the landlord, the tank builder, and the gas company stood in the judicial line together.

However, the chain of causation lacked several links. A 2-year-old fell and needed attention, add him to the rhyme. Mom ran to aid one child, leaving the infant in a sink, put her in, too. A 3-year-old turned on baby's bath with scalding water, the final shackle. Who should have been sued?

Heartless as it sounds, mom's responsible. Toddlers don't know what they're doing. They were under her supervision. Leaving an infant unattended in a sink of water is irresponsible. She knew or should have known the water was scalding hot right out of the tap. She had lived in the apartment for over a year before the accident—and that's all this was—a tragic accident.

Why did this case go to court? The girl didn't want it. She was too young to understand a trial. So her mother probably did it for her, but why? Certainly it was done "for money." In addition, it probably went to court for a mixture of "for justice" and "for principle." She might not have wanted other kids burned; however, as discussed earlier, people seeking justice and principle usually won't take money, at least not beyond medical expenses, legal expenses, and the like.

And what of the defendants, why did they fight? They probably fit into the "for justice" and "for necessity" categories. There was also a tinge of "for obstinacy" and "for intimidation" in their position. They probably thought mom was a guilty party, even though they dared not voice this position for fear of emotional retaliation. A defense attorney would be frightened to argue the mother's negligence because it might inflame the jury. If angered, they could award an incredible amount, although it seems that it couldn't be any more out of line than $15 million.

Sniffing Out The Sue-ers

What drives sue-ers? Lawyers are one side of an equation. The other portion of the formula involves parties, the people who sue others. Parties are like football players. They get down in three-point stances to poke, push, and mangle the opposition. Lawyers only direct their actions, much like a football coach. Attorneys like to think that they are the fighters, the scrappers, the champions. However, lawyers rarely get bloodied in court. That part is reserved for their players. What needs to be considered, if Shakespeare could rethink his famous words, is whether to kill all the litigants. They feed the lawyers, and without them there would be no attorneys.

Unfortunately, people need attorneys desperately today, if for no other reason than to fill their "greed need." We live in a world where the moral of the *Grasshopper and the Ants* is reversed. In the story, the lazy grasshopper thought the world owed him a living, that is until winter came and he nearly froze. Only the vast industry of the ants saved him. He learned his lesson and worked thereafter.

Today, we have the grasshopper's dreams. When Texas
started selling lottery tickets, *USA Today* reported sales of
$23.2 million on the first day they were available. The most
recent census lists the population of the state as less that 17
million. At a buck each, that's more that a ticket for every
person in the state sold in one day. To look for the reason, just
reverse the grasshopper fable—if you win a lottery, your work
is done.

Slot Mania

An example of a *could have been* case involved a retired
traveler who flew from his home to visit his sister in Las
Vegas. On March 17, he boarded a commercial airliner and
settled back for a comfortable return flight when disaster
struck. At 35,000 feet he reached into the seat pocket where
air-sick bags and magazines are kept and was poked by a
bloody syringe that had been left by someone. Also in the
pocket was a wad of stained gauze. The man did what any red-
bloodied American might, he hired a lawyer and sued the
airline for sloppy housekeeping. He fears that he *could have
been* exposed to the AIDS virus. For this fear, he seeks more
than a million dollars. Note that the plaintiff wants that amount
for thinking he might have the virus. Imagine how high his
expectations will be if he actually has it. How ironic that he hit
the right needle in a slot behind a seat while returning from
Nevada on St. Patrick's Day. Oh, the luck of the Irish.

This man is probably going to court for several reasons.
The most obvious is "for money." Like many others, this one
could be for principle or justice, but if it were, the money
would be incidental. The defense is probably going to be "for
obstinacy" and "for intimidation." It's hard to imagine the
defendant seeks to justify leaving dirty syringes around to
stick their patrons.

How much would the plaintiff win for being stuck by a street derelict with an HIV-laden needle? Nothing. However, to pursue a big payoff, his lawyer needs little creativity to form a case of negligence against the airline. The needle was in the pocket, people reach in the pocket, *ergo* the airline is responsible. Because airlines have "deep pockets," the slot behind the seat will pay better than any Vegas machine.

Shot of Pepsi

Syringes aren't confined to airline pouches; they popped up everywhere after an elderly couple in Washington State discovered one in a can of Diet Pepsi. As soon as the media reported the stray needle in the can of cola, errant needles abounded in Pepsi cans as "helpful" citizens called in complaints from dozens of states. In all, there were over 60 tainted cans reported in a couple of weeks

The FDA moved in swiftly, investigated, and referred several of the complaints to the U.S. Attorney's office for prosecution. It seems that most of the findings were copy-cat cases, invented for attention, money, or spite. At least two dozen of the reports have led to arrests for fraudulent reporting of tampered goods.

Why, you might ask, would anyone make a false complaint about a needle in a pop can? Some people will lie for a chance at the tort lottery. It isn't surprising that so many bogus reports came in, but it's shocking that several were caught at their game. With this in mind, just how many cases do you think are on the trial calendar on any given day that are pure fiction? Far too many! Our tort system condones, supports, encourages, and even rewards fraud. However, instead of getting a shot at Pepsi's deep pockets, a few rip-off artists fizzled and could get a peek at Sing-Sing.

A Tragic Crop

The following case appeared in newspapers and some facts were fleshed out by the plaintiff's attorney: A young boy was a popular little-leaguer of considerable maturity. Tall for his age, he was bright and the son of well-educated parents. They believed strongly in giving their son responsibility proportionate to his growth. At age 10, he started cutting the family lawn with a rotary push mower and spent a year mastering the use of it.

A friend had a five-acre parcel and asked if the boy could mow it. The neighbor had a 20-year-old garden tractor that was well maintained by mechanics, however, its brakes were reportedly an inefficient band type. While they would stop the mower as it traveled forward, they were said to be nearly useless when the tractor was in reverse. The boy mowed the lawn under supervision two or three times with no difficulty. Although he was only 11 years old, he was quite competent on the tractor-type mower.

Fate had it in for the youngster. One day he was riding along fine, doing the five-acre parcel solo. He started the mower up a hill, and all the evidence points to the mower stalling on the way up the hill. Without power, it probably started sliding back down the hill. The band brakes were apparently inadequate to hold the tractor as it skidded. Terror must have filled the young boy's heart as the machine backed out of control.

At the foot of the hill was a small pond about 4 feet deep. When the tractor finished its dreadful skid, it flipped over atop the boy, trapping his small frame under water. He struggled in vain. The weight of the machine was more than a match for him, and when he was discovered, he had drowned.

Again, the case is horrible; a boy died, leaving his parents grieving. They did what any self-respecting couple might in similar circumstances, they sued. An urban jury awarded $2.6 million. The boy won't spend any of it. It was only because he died that millions went to his parents. Money enough to catch the greedy eye of many would-be litigants and attorneys.

This case was not brought by the victim—he died—but his right to sue survived. His parents probably went to court in outrage and "for justice." They could have wanted someone to pay, which resembles "for revenge." Most likely they wanted justice, to make the company own up to responsibility.

The defense resembled "for obstinacy," "for intimidation," and "for justice." As discussed before, deep-pocket defendants fight cases with money. They often behave obstinately and use their dollars to intimidate. Corporate defendants are notorious for spending millions for defense, but nothing for tribute.

But, the defendants would also want to show that someone else was at fault for letting a child operate a dangerous machine. This would be "for justice," however, since trials often hinge on emotions instead of on logic, such a defense is dangerous. It's difficult to argue that the parents were responsible for killing their own son. So, while there might have been a "for justice" argument, it's unlikely that it was used.

No Fault

A bright and active 13-year-old boy had just started the eighth grade when tragedy struck. His gym class was scheduled to use the field across the street from the school building for a game of flag football.

To go to the field, the class members needed to cross a busy street. Teachers allowed students to cross without supervision or crossing guards. This Monday morning, a semi-tractor and trailer were said to be parked so close to the crosswalk that they obstructed the northbound view of the street.

The eighth grader was the first of his class to head for the field. A pickup truck was driving slowly down the street, past the crosswalk and just about to pass the parked semi. The boy darted out into the street, apparently without looking, and ran directly into the pickup.

The boy crashed to the asphalt after slamming into the truck. Then he tumbled and stopped breathing. Aid crews revived him and transported him to an emergency care center. Four years later, he survives, but on a gurney. He is quadriplegic and suffers from brain damage. His body requires 24-hour care, and he still is unable to speak. Prognosis for change is poor.

Naturally, the father sued everyone in sight. The shotgun blasted at the school district for letting the students cross the street alone. It aimed at the city for failing to properly mark the road. The barrels poised at the semi-truck, said to be illegally parked. Finally, the chamber cocked upon the driver of the pickup truck. These defendants were negligent, screamed the complaint. All of them must pay. They're at fault.

The jury listened to arguments from all sides during a six-week trial and concluded that the damages were huge. They awarded $345,000 for past economic damages. That covered hospitalization for four years to date. Then, they awarded $5 million for future costs of housing a quadriplegic for the rest of his life. The boy received another $500,000 for pain and suffering. And finally, the jury gave the father half-a-million dollars for loss of companionship and emotional distress.

Those are the numbers we need to work with to do the following math. The jury found each actor partially liable, so none must pay the whole verdict.

They gave the bulk of the liability to the school district, 75 percent. The next chunk went to the semi, 24 percent. The last percent of liability was apportioned one-half percent to another defendant who had ownership interest in the semi, one-quarter percent against the truck driver who hit the boy, and finally one-quarter percent was assessed against the injured student.

Apportioning the fault so precisely seems to say that the jury weighed the facts and shed the blame onto the wrongful actors. Examination of it shows otherwise.

The driver of the truck who hit the boy was one-quarter percent liable. The driver was doing between 20 and 25 MPH when the student darted into the street and hit his truck. How can the driver have any liability? The thought might be: So what, how much is one-quarter percent anyway? When the verdict is $6.3 million, it's almost $16,000. It's incredible that the pickup driver must pay anything to a negligent teenager. If anyone is due money, it's he. What could he have done to avoid the wreck?

The amount of the verdict is offset another one-quarter percent because of the youth's negligence. This says that the student was wrong, but ever so slightly. To get an idea of the incident, consider these statements by witnesses:

One classmate said, "We were heading towards the cross-walk, and [he] ran out in front of a parked diesel that was unloading at the school. As he ran out into the street a Ford truck that was going north on [the] street hit him on the front passenger side of the truck."

Another said, "We were in PE going out to the track. As we were running out towards the track, [he] ran out in front of a parked semi. [We] yelled for him to watch out that there was a truck coming."

Yet another added, "On our way out to the field, [he] ran out into the street in front of a parked semi that was unloading. When he ran out into the street he was hit by a Ford [pickup]."

And finally, one last account. "We were getting ready to go out for flag football and [he] was trying to be the first one out there. I was running behind him. I guess he didn't want to go around the food truck so he ran in front of it. He kinda slowed down to look and then decided to run without looking."

Are those facts upon which a jury should find the student only one-quarter percent liable? Absolutely not. However, when the plaintiff is a quadriplegic, imprisoned on a gurney, the jury feels sorry for him. Since he will forever wear the horrible scars of the accident, he is absolved of responsibility.

This is passion at its height. Either the boy had enough sense not to run into the street, or he didn't. If he didn't, then his parents are responsible for not teaching him about the danger of traffic. If he knew, then he was reckless.

Consideration must be given to whether a 13-year-old boy is responsible enough not to run in front of traffic. In Florida, an 11-year-old boy was allowed to sue his parents for a divorce. We can't have it both ways, either an 11-year-old is incompetent to sue and knows what's best for him, or a 13-year-old knows how to cross a street. Either youths take responsibility for their lives or they don't.

Considering what caused the suit, again we have a plaintiff who could not sue for himself, so his father did it. But why? Did he sue for money? Was it for justice? For principle?

The defendants probably lined up obstinately to intimidate the plaintiff. They certainly used economic muscle to attempt to subdue the litigant. But, once again, they had a strong "for justice" argument. The boy should have known better than to run into the street.

More Flags

A newspaper reported a $9.7 million award for a car-battery explosion. This money went to a good Samaritan who tried to help an elderly couple by jump-starting their car. In the process of the act, the battery exploded in the man's face. He lost an eye and now suffers from seizures. An allegedly defectively-designed battery lacked the proper warning labels to alert the user of danger.

Nine million dollars is a wild flag to wave. Money like that attracts all kinds of people who would never even consider a suit, but for the thought of wealth, money, and greed.

In another case, the *Associated Press* reported a 68-year-old man's life would never be the same after celebrating his 50th wedding anniversary at a restaurant. The party was set in the garden of the inn. Someone noticed wasps around the garbage and the food and complained to the head waiter, who did nothing.

An hour after the warning, a wasp landed on the celebrator's hand and stung him. The toxic bite assaulted the victim's brain stem and spinal cord, plunging the man into a three-week coma. Upon regaining consciousness, he remained paralyzed. The injury he received from the bee sting was terrible. But, the award was bizarre. The jury gave $3.4 million for the sting because the inn was negligent for having wasps there. One-half of the amount was set aside because the man was 50 percent negligent. The net award, according to the newspaper account, was $1.45 million.

If this guy was concerned about some bees, why did he stay at the tavern for an hour after noticing the wasps? He was celebrating his 50th anniversary in the tavern's garden and he wanted to continue the party. Wasn't he assuming a great deal of risk of being stung? Who would he have sued if he had been walking across the street from the inn on his way to pick up a magazine to read? The restaurant because the bee might have come from there? The newsstand for attracting it? The magazine publisher for coaxing him into harm's way? The stupid bee? Where will this stop? The answer is partly that it won't end until lawyers quit sniffing out monster cases, and partly that it won't stop as long as people have a strong "greed need."

Here is a case where the defense would argue strongly "for justice" because they can't control every insect in the county.

Estate Slam Dunk

A high school basketball player was rated as an NBA prospect. In *USA Today,* an article addressed a suit by his estate. A few blocks from school, he reportedly got in a quarrel and was shot. He allegedly lay wounded on a hospital gurney for two hours awaiting surgery, and died of a heart attack during the operation. His family sought $10 million in a lawsuit that they settled eight years after the death for an undisclosed amount. The family attorney was quoted in the article:

> Obviously, there's a monetary settlement; there always is in civil cases. They're happy with it or they would not have made it. But it won't bring [him] back... Basketball talent is unique in that the stars in high school usually go on to be NBA basketball players.

That little quotation, packed with so many problems that have elevated our flawed judicial system to its current crisis, demands analysis. First, consider "there's a monetary settlement." Money and greed can be inferred here. At least the money portion is confirmed in the next clause. "There always is in civil cases." What the attorney stated is the guts of our civil system, the heart of its flaw, the cause of the crisis.

People sue in civil court because they want money. By and large, plaintiffs seek redress dollars. The rare case is filed "for justice" or "for principle." When James Merideth sued to cross the color barrier and attend the University of Mississippi, it was for the principle of the matter. However, the bulk of today's lawsuits look solely for bucks, with only an occasional touch of altruism. This isn't to fault the boy's attorney or his family. Both did what every American considers as a right today, if not an obligation. They went to court for cash. The lawyer did his job well for the family under our present tort system.

The next sentence reads, "They're happy with it or they would not have made it." This quotation is ambiguous because it's difficult to tell who is happy. I assume it means the defendants. In my experience, defendants are rarely *happy* with anything. They were dragged into court and they have little to rejoice over, no matter what the outcome.

It was a poor word choice, but happy is what he said. Defendants are usually miserable throughout the ordeal. From the day they learn of a possible lawsuit, often in a letter from the plaintiff's lawyer, until the matter is put to rest, it is sheer torture. The potential litigation eats away at their innards and steals their sleep. When the inevitable summons and complaint are served, depression mounts.

Throughout the process the defendant spends legal fees to ward off the attack. Often, this is money the party can ill afford. On the other hand, if it's a personal-injury suit for money, the plaintiffs frequently pay no attorney fees because of contingency contracts.

After going through the excruciating process, the case either settles or goes to trial. When it's over, happiness is a total misnomer to describe the emotions felt by the parties. Relief might better express it. Hate, vengeance, anger, and contempt could also be used in most cases. We developed our legal system to settle disputes, but it works far better at breeding hatred and unrest. It's a rare defendant who walks away from the courtroom happy.

The next sentence says, "But it won't bring him back." This is the classic legal ploy for sympathy. Of course it won't bring back the high schooler. Our system is imperfect, and not at all godlike. It never raises from the dead. In fact, it thrives on the opposite. All our system can do is make some people involved so miserable that it ruins their health or kills them.

Plaintiff's lawyers love to say, "No matter what you do, it won't bring this person back to life." It's the ultimate guilt trip and should be barred from the courtroom. It's designed solely to inflame the passions of whoever hears it. Prosecuting attorneys use it to try to inspire jurors to convict a killer. They know the force of the words. The words play on emotions, not on facts. Personal-injury attorneys use the words to jack-up an award beyond reason. Cases should be built on facts, not emotions.

The final statement made by the lawyer was: "Basketball talent is unique in that the stars in high school usually go on to be NBA basketball players." What in the world does this mean? That this boy's death is worse than another's because he could put a ball in a hoop? A death is a death. Friends and family alike mourn the loss of a loved one, especially when the person is still in high school. One must infer from the statement that because of potential, the family deserves more money. What he didn't earn on one court, his family cleans up in another. That's lunacy. It shouldn't matter whether he was talented or not. All that matters is that he's dead.

Who Needs The Sue-ers?

Many people say, "Who cares about all these suits?" The answer is that the lawyers do. They thrive on them by filing 50,000 new suits a day. But the litigation is crippling the rest of the country.

While some sue-ers argue that lawsuits bring about noble changes and make the world a better place, consider this brief counter-argument. In a country alleged to be the most litigious in the world, neighbors sued for pennies and spite. They went to court for everything because the courts condoned petty disputes. If excessive filing of lawsuits were good for public harmony, this country must have been the most "civil" in the world. The country in question is the former Yugoslavia.

CHAPTER 7

Catch And Release

The public sees the criminal justice system as a swinging door where crooks go free almost as soon as they are arrested. It's perceived that the rules are stacked against the police, and they might as well be fishing in a catch-and-release lake where every fish caught must be set free for another angler to land. The dominant theme of the swinging jailhouse door is that court rulings let too many villains go free on technicalities. The following discussion concerns the *Miranda* "technicality":

Burgy tripped a wire as he pried a window open to enter a store. The shop owner suspected someone had been entering the premises at night. A newly installed system triggered an alert to the police. After Burgy helped himself to merchandise, he turned to exit through the window. The lights in the store flipped on and staring at him was the bore of a .357-magnum revolver aimed at his nose. The officer, clenching the gun with both hands, yelled, "Freeze!"

Realizing there was trouble, Burgy dropped the goods and hoisted his hands high. Proud of the collar, the constable handcuffed the thief and put him in a police car. In the jail, the following conversation took place:

Cop: I've never seen you before and the computer says you got no record. Have you ever been arrested before?
Burgy: No, I've never been to a police station.
Cop: What are you stealing comic books for?
Burgy: Should I tell you?
Cop: Of course, I'm here to help you.
Burgy: I collect them.
Cop: How'd you get in?
Burgy: A window.
Cop: You break in there before?
Burgy: Three times last month.
Cop: Always for comics?
Burgy: Yeah, I'm out of work, can't afford them, you know.

Anyone who ever watched a police show knows the officer blew it. He didn't start the interview with the infamous *Miranda* warning about constitutional rights. Burgy should have been informed before any interrogation commenced:

You have the right to remain silent. Anything you say can be used against you in a court of law. You have the right to have an attorney present during questioning. If you cannot afford legal counsel, you will be appointed one to represent you at no cost to you. Should you decide to answer questions at this time, you have the right to stop answering at any time. Do you understand these rights? Do you wish to waive these rights?

Police give these warnings because the courts insist upon it. The leading case is *Miranda v. Arizona,* in which Chief Justice Earl Warren wrote the landmark opinion from the bench of the U.S. Supreme Court. That case said that the U.S. Constitution grants certain rights, even to criminals.

The Fifth Amendment includes several rights, one of them being: "...nor shall any person... be compelled in any criminal case to be a witness against himself..." In the Sixth Amendment is the dictate that "the accused shall... have the assistance of counsel..."

Justice Warren said that the prosecution must honor certain procedural requirements or they can't use statements taken from a defendant who was interrogated while in custody. *Being in custody means to be deprived of freedom. It's a critical element because the police have total control of the situation and it's easy to coerce a confession.* Once the accused is in custody, he must be told he need not talk.

Ill-gotten statements face rejection in court because police and prosecutors are sometimes overzealous. Courts must guard the public from law enforcement personnel whose desire for conviction overrides the rule of law. Confessions must be voluntarily given or they are inadmissible.

It would offend almost anyone's sense of decency to allow as evidence any statements made after a baton beating by Los Angeles Police. Assume that after massive pummeling, Rodney King finally relented and said: "Yes, I did it—I did it!" Under the circumstances, King might have said anything to have the bludgeoning stop. His confession would have been involuntary—tainted and unusable in court.

One need not be pummeled to be forced into making a statement. Another abhorrent tactic is sleep deprival. In the novel *Darkness at Noon*, the author describes how persecutors in the old Soviet Union would badger suspects for hours on end with bright lights. Inspectors moved prisoners in and out of their cells so frequently that sleep was impossible. Finally, when totally disoriented, suspects crumbled and admitted to anything just for some sleep and repose.

While those are the most severe types of police behavior that must be avoided, there are other more subtle ones. Psychological warfare is waged against any suspect who is being questioned. The police have all the power. They control the events and the area where interrogations take place. Judges fear that police will coerce confessions in these overwhelmingly one-sided interviews. Not only because they abhor coercive tactics used to extract statements, but also because those types of admissions are unreliable.

This brings us back to the *Miranda* decision, which is the butt of vast criticism. It's commonly believed that if the constable blunders by asking any questions before giving the magic warnings, the crook goes free. That belief is totally false.

The erroneous assumption bombards the public. Television shows it and newspapers write about it. It's told on the radio and talked about on the street. The reasons behind much of the belief are bias, ignorance, or sloppy journalism.

In a typical case, a reporter learns that a confession has been ruled inadmissible by the court. The case is so weak that its success hinges on the admission of guilt by the defendant. Therefore, the prosecuting attorney dismisses the charges rather than fight a hopeless battle. Our faithful reporter writes a headline that declares another crook is freed because of a technical error. In reality, the defendant went free because the case against him fell apart unless the prosecutor used an illegally obtained statement.

In the article, the reader might discover that our system values the right to remain silent. He might even learn that in old England the Star Chamber and the ecclesiastical courts extorted confessions—a tactic that the Founding Fathers banned from our legal system. He could read that Americans are protected by the Constitution from being tortured. However, it's unlikely that any of that would appear in the story. It doesn't make good copy. It doesn't sell newspapers.

What appears in the paper is a prejudicial account of a horrible crime that will go unpunished because a police officer made a mistake. A single incident is used to spur anger and to sell papers. People remember the message that criminals are freed on technicalities. In truth, the suspect was freed because the police had little or no proof without the confession. It was a feeble case that required an ill-gotten statement to support it.

An example of what I consider inflammatory reporting appeared in the *National Review*. The article discussed a case where an escapee from jail admitted killing two people in a mobile home. The confession was discarded because a lawyer wasn't present during the interrogation. Discussing why the Supreme Court threw out the statement, the writer claims that the *Miranda* rule stretches beyond reason, and that the police won't get confessions from "anyone who is not perversely determined to establish his own guilt." It closes with a message that reveals its slant:

> Conservatives had hoped that three Reagan-appointed Justices would be enough to deflect the Court from such proceduralism gone mad. In vain. Too bad the people in the mobile home didn't have a lawyer present when they were killed.

The writer used an impassioned ending to inflame the reader. His message was that conservatives hoped all procedural rights of persons accused of crimes would diminish under Reagan's conservative appointees to the Supreme Court. The problem is that a right based upon the Constitution *isn't* a technicality. That document is the foundation of our entire legal system.

In an expansive essay titled *Ideology and Criminal Rights*, Paul Savoy portrays the following case as an example of how our criminal justice system protects the guilty:

A person was convicted for killing a teenage girl and sentenced to die in the electric chair. The young girl's brains were spattered about while someone bludgeoned her head with a 44-pound boulder.

The convicted killer sat on death row for 14 years before the United States Supreme Court threw out his confession of guilt. He had been questioned under coercive circumstances and had not been advised of his right to remain silent or his right to legal representation. The court decided that ten hours of interrogation without receiving any warning was too much.

Denied of the use of the illegally obtained confession, the prosecution was unable to go forward in a new trial. Their case depended upon the admission of guilt. Other than the confession, the proof was flimsy. Without the confession there was insufficient evidence to prove the accused had murdered the girl. Although originally professing guilt, the defendant staunchly pleaded innocence thereafter. Five years after his release on the charge, while on trial for an unrelated charge of kidnapping and attempted murder, the man reconfessed to the earlier killing. At least the man was convicted of the new charges.

It appears that Savoy wants the reader to think that someone got away with murder. His argument disregards that a person who sat on death row 14 years has received 14 years of punishment. If the person had served less time, Savoy's argument would have been stronger. He also ignores the fact that many states parole murderers after 13 years. Finally, the author forgets that a confession may be given for several reasons, not all of which point toward guilt. The confessor could have been mentally deranged and only thought he committed the crime. He could have been shielding a friend or relative.

Either of those reasons point toward unreliable statements. Unfortunately, the issue that the article drives home is that a heinous act occurred and the killer got off free.

The most convincing argument against giving criminals Miranda rights is that some crooks get away with murder. I can't deny that—some bad guys go free because of the Bill of Rights. What must be considered is that most people who are charged with a crime are convicted. Very few slip through the net, but it is those few that everyone hears about.

We can tighten the mesh of the net and let fewer escape, but the cost will be that more innocent people will go to jail. If we allow police to beat confessions out of suspects, we'll get more blameless people confessing for another's crime. If you saw the Rodney King beating tape, you know that police can be brutal. Also, if we encourage police to psychologically manipulate the people they have in custody, there will be more admissions by defendants.

It's an age-old dilemma: Do we attempt to convict every criminal, regardless of how many lambs we slaughter? Personally, I would rather see a few crooks go free than innocent people jailed. It's a price that we have to pay. The majority of our Founding Fathers concurred; that's why they attached the Bill of Rights to the Constitution—to protect the innocent.

As I indicated earlier, it is untrue that killers walk away from valid charges because of improper questioning by the police. Criminals don't win unless the prosecution's case is weak without the statement. The remedy for an officer taking a confession without first appraising the defendant of his right to keep quiet is suppression of the statement. That's all. It means that a confession obtained illegally because it didn't conform to *Miranda* is inadmissible in court. It doesn't let any crooks off if there is a good case against them!

Prove It!

Cases are developed based upon *evidence*, a word that lawyers use to mean almost anything that can legally be presented to the jury. Evidence is specifically limited to whatever is shown to the *trier of fact*, (usually the judge or the jury that hears a case and decides what the facts are). It might be verbal, written, or otherwise recorded. Even the mannerisms of the witnesses as they testify are evidence. Whatever jurors see, sense, touch, smell, hear, or taste during the trial is evidence or proof of the case. The critical circumstance is that it must be admissible in court.

If the court rejects an illegally obtained confession, the police are in no different position than if they decided not to talk to the suspect. They must have enough evidence to slam the defendant without the illegal confession. Likewise, their case is as strong as it would be if they had given the warnings and the defendant refused to waive his rights.

In both cases, the police must go forward without a confession. The main difference is that if police obtain an illegal confession, they know they have the crook. After that, the focus of their investigation centers on him, and they're bound to turn up more evidence to implicate the accused. In this way, our police are rewarded for breaking the law.

An example of this is shown in a case that baffled police for decades. Twenty years ago, a young man died of a gun-shot wound. At the time, police questioned the victim's friends and searched the scene to no avail. For 16 years the case was unsolvable.

Then someone's sense of guilt broke the silence. A fellow went to the police station and confessed to killing his brother. The officer thought the confessor was "vague, confused and disoriented," and let him go free. It was a correct call by the policeman. The guilt-ridden man never had a brother.

Later, the same fellow confessed to killing a friend. The confession was made to a detective who had questioned him about the homicide 16 years earlier. According to defense counsel, part of the confession talked about the type of ammunition used in the slaying. The police believed that the bullets were "wad cutters," which leave a clean hole in the victim. The confessor kept insisting the bullets were round-nosed reloads.

The police didn't like this information because it conflicted with their theory of the case. They unsuccessfully attempted to change the confessor's opinion of the type of bullets used. Finally, ballistics tests were redone on the bullets; the results showed the bullets to be re-loads and not wad cutters. The case began to take form and the veracity of the statement by the man who claimed to have killed a non-existent brother was improving.

After the admission was made to the police, they directed their efforts toward convicting the confessor. Working on the new theory, the case went to trial and the confession was admitted as part of the prosecution's evidence. A jury convicted. Without the statement, there was virtually no evidence to implicate the defendant. The defense appealed with the hope of having the confession thrown out by a higher court. Even if the statement is obliterated by an appellate court, the police believe in the guilt of the accused and will relentlessly search for independent evidence of his guilt.

For argument, assume that the appeal succeeds. Should the case be re-tried without the confession, the matter will rise or fall on the other evidence. He won't go free just because the admission of guilt is ruled to have been illegally obtained. The defendant will go free only if the rest of the prosecution's case is so tenuous that it can't prevail.

The preceding matters were actual events. A hypothetical burglary opened this analysis. The reason for using imagined facts is that actual cases frequently have complicating factors to muddy the legal reasoning. A mythical matter can be presented to exactly define the issue. In Burgy's case, he will be convicted despite the officer's failure to give *Miranda* warnings. He was caught in the act. Those facts don't change regardless of procedural blunders committed in obtaining the confession.

Burgy's statement is inadmissible. He was in custody and questioned before being advised to keep quiet. The confession was illegally obtained. Taking it violated Burgy's right to be free from "self-incrimination." The constable must find evidence independent of the statement that Burgy was the crook. Since the store owner lacked proof of earlier burglaries there could be no showing of the three prior incidents without the use of the confession. Burgy will win those three cases and lose the one where he was caught in the act. The police are in the same position as if no questions had been asked.

Courts demand that an accused person receive an unequivocal warning of the right to remain silent and the right to assistance of a lawyer. According to studies, these warnings haven't materially affected the conviction rates. Like most other warnings, they are generally disregarded by the recipients.

Criminals being interrogated hear the officer start to give the message. The suspect often parrots the language they heard from a previous arrest, or from listening to it on television. Usually the words have no meaning to the suspects. They are in such a frightening situation that everything goes over their head. Sounds make words, but the words fail to register. The stressful situation depletes human reasoning power. Even under the best of circumstances, many people don't know that to waive means to give up something.

A study conducted in New Haven, Connecticut, concluded that the warnings had little effect for two reasons: First, the police rarely arrested someone without having substantial evidence of guilt. Second, few suspects exercised the right to silence. They talked even after being advised to shut their mouths.

In a larger city, a study showed a 20 percent decline in confessions obtained from suspects, but no change in the conviction rate. The conclusion of *Miranda in Pittsburgh—A Statistical Study,* was that "Miranda has not impaired significantly the ability of law enforcement agencies to apprehend and convict the criminal."

Again, we have precautions with no substance. Only a few receive any protection from the warnings. Those who exercised their rights usually knew of the dangers of talking before the interrogation. They got this knowledge from previously being in the criminal system, or from advice of a professional. Usually, the warnings go unheeded.

If our courts really wanted to protect the right to remain silent, they would declare that all custodial confessions, regardless of the circumstances, were inadmissible. Although admissions against interest are frequently unreliable, the courts don't want to ban their use in trial. Instead they're satisfied if a hollow warning established the procedural requirement.

Like in many other aspects of our system, procedure is more important than substance. Innocent people can be convicted if the proper procedure is followed. Guilty ones are released if improper technique is employed. It's not what was done that concerns our courts, but how it was accomplished. We don't seem to care what is right, as long as it's done properly. It's a flaw brought about by judicial infatuation with warnings and words.

More Technicalities

Discussion of the *Miranda* rule covers but one of the many "technicalities" in our system. Numerous technicalities are packed into our Bill of Rights. Some of the fundamental technicalities include:

1. Freedom of Religion;
2. Free Speech;
3. Right to Bear Arms;
4. Freedom from Unreasonable Searches and Seizures;
5. Right to Remain Silent;
6. Protection Against Double Jeopardy;
7. Right to Due Process of the Law;
8. Right to a Speedy Trial in Criminal Matters;
9. Right to an Impartial Jury in Criminal Matters;
10. Right to Confront Witnesses in Criminal Matters;
11. Right to A Lawyer in Criminal Matters;
12. Right to a Jury Trial in Civil Cases;
13. Protection from Cruel and Unusual Criminal Punishment.

Take notice how many fundamental technicalities are granted us in the Bill of Rights for the protection from criminal persecution. Of all the rights listed above, only the right to a have a jury hear civil matters is totally divorced from the criminal justice system. However, the right to a jury trial is so fundamental to fair treatment in the criminal procedure that I included it in the list above. When our country revolted, our Founding Fathers were fearful of government oppression. They passed the Bill of Rights and built this country upon the principle that liberty and freedom were the most important aspects of life.

It is by virtue of these protections granted in the Bill of Rights that nearly every technicality has developed to protect criminals from the hangman. While nobody wants to willingly grant these technicalities to the likes of Ted Bundy, it is only by granting him those rights that we can assure ourselves that they will be intact for us.

This isn't to suggest that we need to be soft on criminals, or make it impossible to convict them. On the contrary, criminals must be given swift and certain punishment for their misdeeds. However, we want criminals arrested, tried, convicted, and sentenced within the scope of the law. This can be done fairly and justly. We don't need the LAPD viciously pummeling suspects any more than we want crooks getting away with murder. And once someone is convicted, they shouldn't be allowed unending appeals. There is a balance that must be made between protection of a criminal's rights and protection of society. As we become stricter in criminal procedure, freedom is sacrificed.

Consider this recent case: A bus was stopped in Florida and passengers were asked to consent to being searched for drugs. A man consented to the search and illegal drugs were discovered in his possession. The United States Supreme Court upheld the search as reasonable. It indicated that anyone could say "no" to the police request, but if they consented, the search was valid.

Most people would say, "Who cares. Drug dealers need to be stopped." The problem is this: Now that police know they can stop a bus full of people and "ask" them to display their wares, they probably will. People will consent to these searches because of respect for the law. The searches might even become a routine part of traveling on buses. We already allow electronic searches of our bags and persons at airports. The reason for doing so is valid; it stops some hijacking attempts. However, whenever we protect ourselves from crooks in this way, we give up our freedom. It is a trade-off. How often is a bus hijacked? Do we need to search its passengers?

Even more so, consider what will happen in the following hypothetical case: Beth is a middle-aged woman riding with her elderly aunt on a bus. The aunt has a poor memory and suffers from chronic back pain. Her physician prescribed strong narcotics. Beth removed them from their huge prescription bottle and placed them into a compact travel case in her purse. When their bus was stopped, Beth allowed the constable to search her bag and he found a month's supply of opiate. Beth was busted. She technically violated the law by taking the medicine out of its original container. If the police want to, they can take Beth to jail.

Protection against unreasonable searches and seizures are there for people like Beth. While it is true that some crooks are released because of "bad searches," consider the *Miranda* example. If the police have a good case without the illegally obtained evidence, the crook is still busted.

Although some people believe it would be nice to strip thieves of their rights, it's hard to tell the guilty from the innocent at first blush. That's why everyone gets the same treatment and equal protection.

Lest you think that government would never persecute individuals who exercised their "technical" rights, remember the Salem witch trials, where at least 19 people were hanged for practicing witchcraft. This was done in a colony that was formed by Pilgrims who fled England to escape religious persecution. Those who were hanged would be protected today by the Freedom of Religion clause of the First Amendment.

And when Senator McCarthy chased down Communists in every crevice, those people *should* have been protected by free speech. Unfortunately, when people have power, they sometimes become enamored with it and abuse it. The Bill of

Rights helps check the state from oppressing its citizens. If we wish to discard any of its "technicalities," we must do so with an open mind, and fully aware of the consequences.

At this point, I would like you to turn back and review the rights listed earlier in this section. Take a pen and draw a line through each "technicality" that you would like to see abolished. Then, you will be on the road to a benign government's utopia, provided the people in power remain altruistic.

But do you really want to take that risk?

Let's Make A Deal

Plea bargaining is thought of as a contemptible technicality by most Americans. It's the invisible process where prosecuting attorneys agree to reduce charges or offer light sentences in order to extract guilty pleas from defendants. Like anything done in the back rooms, it's highly suspect. On the surface, it gives the appearance of sacrificing public safety by treating criminals lightly. To many, it represents the worst flaw in our judicial system. People see it as the ultimate hypocrisy where lawyers pretend to hate one another yet negotiate away all manner of crimes while compromising community standards.

The arguments against plea bargaining are that it's secretive, forges a partnership between cops and crooks, and punishes "bad guys" unequally. There are no rebuttals to these. They can only be tempered with an explanation of why plea bargaining is a necessary evil, at least temporarily.

To offset the rationale against plea bargaining, consider the following: Sometimes leniency is offered for reasons unapparent to the casual observer. It could be that the state's case is weak. Also, the court calendar might be so crowded that if one matter is tried, a more serious case must be dismissed. There are only so many prosecutors in an office and a limited number of courts. When a criminal doesn't get a speedy hearing date, the charges must be dismissed under our Constitution. Many other factors can affect the decision for the prosecutor to offer leniency in exchange for a guilty plea.

While preparing this portion of the book, I spoke with the prosecuting attorney of a large county who often speaks out in behalf of plea bargaining. One analogy he uses is that plea bargaining is like a hammer and can be either a tool of construction or one of destruction. It can build a house or kill a person. However, the hammer itself can't be bad, only the user can be.

One case he discusses in support of plea bargaining involved brutal beatings a young boy suffered at the hands of his father. These were no ordinary thrashings; the toddler was abused regularly, until one whipping finally killed him. In order to secure a conviction of the assailant, the prosecutor needed the testimony of the boy's mother. She received leniency because of a plea bargain. Without the bargain for testimony, the killer might have gone free. Instead, the father was convicted of murder and sentenced to 60 years in prison.

Although that case supports plea bargains, what happened in the following one? A man charged with tax fraud was allowed to plead *nolo contendere* to a charge of tax evasion. Nolo contendere means "no contest" and works like a guilty plea except the defendant never admits guilt. This party might also have been charged with bribery and extortion if he didn't plea bargain. At sentencing, the prosecutor successfully argued to the judge for the defendant to receive probation rather than prison because he had suffered enough by resigning his government post and deserved leniency. The judge said he would have sent the defendant to jail without the prosecutor's argument for probation. The recipient of plea-bargaining largess was Spiro Agnew.

Bargains are often necessary when there are multiple defendants. Consider the Rodney King beating trials. Prosecutors had a terrible time making a case because there were so many police officers who said, "You got it wrong, it happened this way." The more defendants stick together, the tougher it is to convict them. If there are to be any convictions in cases with several defendants, it's often imperative that a plea bargain be struck with the least culpable actors in exchange for their testimony against the more heinous ones.

Statistics on plea bargains are unreliable, but most experts agree that approximately 90 percent of all convictions come from pleas of guilty. Only 10 percent are from verdicts of the court or jury. For misdemeanors, it's believed that only 5 percent of the convictions come after trial. There are several reasons for this: mainly, because most people charged with crimes are guilty of some wrong-doing. The issue isn't whether we have a "bad guy," but to determine what crime is appropriate.

Like many aspects of our legal system, the plea bargain is a complex mechanism. It involves the relinquishment of several rights by the defendant in exchange for leniency. Herein is a plan to remedy the perceived and actual inequities of the system. Bear in mind that the changes presented are radical and expensive.

The focus of plea bargaining rests squarely on the prosecuting attorney. While defense lawyers all participate, there would be none if prosecutors refused to negotiate. However, all the blame can't be shoved upon district attorneys. They inherited a system from the British, which gives them monstrous amounts of discretion. A prosecutor is allowed to evaluate the facts of a case, consider what crimes apply to those facts, and charge whatever they please. Likewise, district attorneys can dismiss or reduce charges at will.

In order to halt plea bargaining, prosecuting attorneys would have to relinquish their total discretion to charge at will. They could be forced to take the cases to independent magistrates who would evaluate the facts and order the prosecutor to try the case as deemed appropriate. The prosecutor couldn't negotiate with the defense because there would be no power to do so.

While this might sound like an ideal solution, consider the cost. Ninety percent of all defendants plead guilty today because they were granted concessions from the prosecutors. When the district attorneys have no power to negotiate, many defendants will opt for a jury trial. They will be treated the same whether they plead guilty or not guilty, so most defendants will roll the dice in the courtroom, hoping for a favorable verdict.

Under the current system, criminal defendants go to trial, but not often. Without plea bargains, many defendants would refuse to plead guilty. If represented by competent counsel, they would demand a trial on the charges because they would have little to lose, except for legal fees. However, most people charged with felonies are represented by court-appointed lawyers because they can't afford to pay an attorney. For them, there is no financial benefit in pleading guilty, and excellent reasons to have a trial. They could win an acquittal and be cleared of the charges outright, or the court docket could be so crowded that their case would be dismissed for want of timely prosecution. Even if they lose, they can appeal the decision; there is virtually no right to appeal from a guilty plea. Nearly everyone would want a trial. In fact, it would probably be malpractice for a defense attorney to allow a client to plead guilty.

To get an idea of what this would mean, multiply all of the current trials by ten. The prosecutor I spoke of earlier said that in 1992, 8.9 percent of his office's cases went to trial and that his staff was working at full-capacity. He guessed that to eliminate plea bargaining, both he and the public defender would need a ten-fold increase in budgets to try all the cases.

In addition, the police force would need to grow. With every case going to trial, officers would sit in court all day waiting to testify instead of attending to their duties on the streets.

Beyond the economic costs are other concerns. With more trials, a greater number of crooks will be acquitted—the law of averages will take care of that. And witnesses would be forced into the trauma of testifying, facing their assailants, and reliving frightful acts, which is often avoided with pleas of guilty.

Additionally, our prisons are bursting with inmates and court calenders are so crowded that cases can take months or years to get a hearing. Without plea bargains, we would be forced into building a plethora of courtrooms and jails, hiring an army of prosecutors and their defensive counterparts, and increasing the police forces dramatically.

Currently, criminal matters involve 40 percent of all trials in federal courts. This is despite only 16 percent of all cases filed in federal courts are criminal. In 1989, 87 percent of all convictions were from guilty pleas. Most can be assumed to have occurred through plea bargaining. Had every criminal case gone to trial in 1989, the entire civil docket would have been ignored and still more than half the criminal cases would have been dismissed for want of a courtroom. If trials were held on every criminal charge, courts would bulge, then sputter, and finally cease to function.

Plea bargaining is a flaw in our system, but it is a flaw of necessity, at least for the short term. Our jails are bursting. We have so many convicts incarcerated, we can't add another inmate without releasing one or building another jail. Likewise, court dockets are screaming for relief.

To end plea bargaining, it must be done gradually. Otherwise, there would be chaos. It can be done if we relegate the prosecutor to an arm of the law with a single function—that is to present cases to the court and try them. With the discretion removed, there could be no bargains struck.

This "solution" must be tempered with the thought of its cost. It would be a boon to everyone in the criminal justice system. That branch of government would swell—perhaps tenfold. In our quest to treat every thief and pervert equally, the taxpayer would be saddled with an enormous bill.

Real Technicalities

Not all technicalities are critical to freedom. There are some that deserve little or no respect, and likewise, no protection. My state once had a speedy trial provision in the court rules that must have been designed for crooks.

The rule said that a criminal must be brought to trial within 60 days if in custody and 90 days if out of jail; if not, their case was dismissed. When a defendant appeared before a judge, a trial date was set. If the court *accidentally* set the case beyond the mandated rules, defense attorneys quietly sat, waiting for the date to pass. Then, the attorney would move for a dismissal on the grounds that the defendant had been *denied* a speedy trial, and the crook went free.

This rule idiotically applied strict procedure that freed many "bad guys" because of clerical errors. I won several cases because someone in the court system miscounted the days, and set the trial a day too late. This isn't justice; it's lunacy. A person accused of a crime needs a speedy trial so they won't sit in the dungeon for years waiting for the government to invent a charge. Speedy trials shield defendants from abuse, but it's ridiculous to let minor miscalculations free murderers. My state corrected this flawed procedural problem by requiring defendants to object if they didn't think they were receiving a speedy trial. Once the objection was voiced, the court corrected the counting error.

The discussion above is a true "technicality" that should not be encouraged or honored. We need to purge any such "technicalities" from the system. All they do is defeat justice, raise contempt for courts, and free crooks. While we should cautiously guard our fundamental rights, there is no need to contrive traps for the unwary.

CHAPTER 8

Warning:
Read With Caution

While splashing *Fabergé Brut* on my face recently, a small set of white letters on the green bottle intrigued me. As the cologne bit into pores left open from a warm shower and a shave, I read:

CAUTION: FLAMMABLE UNTIL DRY. DO NOT USE NEAR FIRE, FLAME OR HEAT.

Having used the same lotion for 15 years, it surprised me that the warning had gone unnoticed. It crossed my mind as I reviewed the warning that I was being taken for an imbecile. Of course it was flammable. If its morning sting didn't alert me, the "SD Alcohol 39-C" listed on the bottle as the most prevalent ingredient surely would. Flambé deserts dance with a blue flame from lit brandy. Automobiles run on it. Oil companies market gasohol. It ignites; it's an age-old heat source. While considering the warning label, I pulled several bottles out of the medicine cabinet and found many statements of pending peril.

My daughter's hair spray bottles displayed similar warnings. *Focus 21* said, "CAUTION: Flammable. Do not use near open flame or while smoking."

Salon Selectives by *Helene Curtis* said, "**WARNING:** Contents Flammable. Avoid fire, flame or smoking during use and until hair is thoroughly dry."

Bold Hold stated, "**CAUTION:** CONTENTS FLAMMABLE. DO NOT USE NEAR FIRE OR OPEN FLAME. KEEP AWAY FROM MATCHES AND LIGHTED CIGARETTES DURING APPLICATION AND UNTIL HAIR IS FULLY DRY."

Rave 2 Super Hold proclaimed, "**WARNING: FLAMMABLE.** AVOID FIRE, FLAME, HEAT, AND SMOKING DURING APPLICATION AND UNTIL HAIR IS THOROUGHLY DRY."

The main ingredient in all of the sprays was alcohol. My curiosity aroused, I imagined bizarre circumstances that might have led to these warning labels on the vials. In an updated Marx Brothers' movie, Groucho might spray *Focus 21* at soup as it boiled on a gas range to give it body. Harpo could puff *Rave* vapor at a wreath hanging over a fireplace to keep its boughs from falling. Chico might squirt *Salon Selectives* on a lighted birthday cake to keep the icing from dripping.

After visualizing hair-spray absurdities, I contemplated how perfume might cause the same type of warning label to be applied. A fool might splash *Brut* on their electric heater to freshen the room before dousing a lit cigarette with it to make incense.

All these seemed ridiculous. Logic suggests that liability couldn't possibly attach to a manufacturer for such idiotic uses of their product. Assuming that the actual reason for the warnings would be mundane, I stalked the law library in search of the judicial wizard responsible for the labels. There lay the case of the wanton cologne. In the stacks of cases lay a judicial decision that triggered these, and many other warnings.

Decades ago, a group of adolescents congregated at a home for a party. Among the teenagers invited were a 17-year-old girl I'll call Georgia Burns and her 15-year-old friend I'll call Getcha Allen. Most of the people went outside, leaving Burns and Allen alone in the basement. Boredom overtook the young ladies. In quest of entertainment, they noticed a burning Christmas-tree-shaped candle. Sniffing for fragrance and discovering none, Allen applied her teen talent. "Well, let's make it scented," she said while impulsively grabbing a "drip bottle" of *Fabergé's Tigress Cologne* and allegedly pouring its contents onto the candle. According to her own testimony, Burns stood nearby, bewildered by her friend's actions. She claimed little or no responsibility. When the alcohol in the cologne met the open flame, an instantaneous burst of fire sprang onto Burns, searing her neck and breasts.

Since Burns was a minor, her father took on the parental task of suing for his daughter. Daddy lifted a judicial scattergun, and let it loose. He sued Allen for causing the eruption that sprayed fire on Burns, and the host who owned the home where the bomb exploded. As an apparent afterthought, he amended his charges to include *Fabergé* for failing to warn about the product's inherent danger.

Taking the best interpretation of the facts, the teenagers were playing scientist, mixing ingredients while applying heat in hopes of discovering a new air freshener. As they sniffed their experiment, it sprung fire on Burns.

Burns testified that she knew about scented candles, but had never heard of anyone perfuming one. She also stated that she didn't know what Allen poured on the candle and was ignorant of the ingredients in cologne. However, she admitted that you don't pour unknown chemicals on flames. In other words, she knew better than to play with fire.

Contained in the law of torts is the doctrine of *proximate cause*. Simplified, it is an interpretation of someone's action or inaction to determine whether that person caused the injury. If a person is the proximate cause of a mishap, then they are responsible for it. Courts examine accidents in search of the culpable parties. Sometimes more than one person is in the chain. In this case, the sequence goes something like this:

The host invited the adolescents over and left them alone with a candle and perfume. When the jury was asked if this was a proximate cause of the injury to Burns, they said it wasn't. He was not a proximate cause of it; hence, he was legally blameless.

Ms. Allen blended the candle and cologne until she created a flame-throwing bomb. The jury also answered "no" to the following question: "Do you find the defendant Getcha Allen guilty of negligence proximately causing the injury to Georgia Burns?" She was innocent and not a proximate cause of the fire.

After similarly releasing Burns of all responsibility, the jury poised for the attack. They found that *Fabergé* was the sole proximate cause of the injury because they failed to warn of the inherent dangerousness of cologne. A verdict of $27,000 was awarded to Burns, and about one-tenth as much to her father.

What was the theory for finding the manufacturer guilty of negligence? It's always a guess as to what any jury thought about as they deliberated their verdict. Unless members of the jury tell someone, it's a secret. There was an experiment to eavesdrop on the deliberation process to study the workings of juries, but it was discarded almost as soon as it began.

We can speculate that the jury decided it would be unfortunate to make Burns' friends pay for the injury. If that's the case, the jury didn't understand human behavior. There's nothing that a person can do to another that's much worse than subjecting them to the worry and misery of a lawsuit. Any friendship they had went into the waste bin when the suit hit the parties.

Possibly the jury went after the manufacturer because they have so much money that a verdict is of little consequence. Whatever the reason, the jury's decision was against *Fabergé*.

We Never, Never Give Up

Fabergé moved the court for judgment notwithstanding the verdict. It is a motion that is rarely successful. Courts try to leave jury verdicts undisturbed. However, the trial judge thought that it was inconceivable that the use of the cologne would be to perfume a lit candle, so he set aside the jury's decision. This had the effect of reversing the jury verdict. It said that as a matter of law, *Fabergé* was blameless. Burns had won and then lost. She appealed to a higher court, and lost again because:

> There was a total absence of… a rational inference that Fabergé foresaw or should have foreseen that its cologne would be used in the manner which caused the injuries to Georgia Burns. Since Fabergé did not foresee the use, it had no duty to warn against it.

Burns was out of luck because she undertook a dangerous activity and used the product for something far outside the realm of imagination. There are plenty of appellate courts in this country, and Burns wanted a win. If a party has enough money, time, and patience, the case can drag on for years. When she lost the appeal, she cried to a higher court. This one agreed with the jury and Burns became the ultimate victor.

The appellate court considered a treatise lawyers fall back on when there is no case law to support their position. It's called the *Restatement Second, Torts*. In that writing is the guidance for our current warning-label mania. Section 388 of the Restatement contains several sentences of legalese that mean:

Whoever should expect an item to be *dangerous* in its *probable use* and supplies it to someone else is liable if:

(a) he has reason to know of the danger in the use, AND

(b) he has no reason to believe the user would realize its danger, AND

(c) he fails to use reasonable care in *warning* them.

The section seems to say that liability stretches to the intended uses of a product, and not beyond. The appellate court wanted to extend the responsibility to the manufacturer of the cologne, so they went into analysis of other cases and developed a doctrine of foreseeable uses within a general field of danger. They said that it didn't really matter whether *Fabergé* foresaw the crazy use by the teenagers. The important issue was that the manufacturer knew that alcohol burned, and that cologne could be exposed to flame.

The *Restatement* clearly says manufacturers are liable for *probable* uses of their products. To get around this, the court incorporated mental gymnastics to reach the decision. If a court wants to expand the current law, they use legal reasoning and push the actual language of the statute beyond its usual meaning.

The court reasoned that they wouldn't hold a shoemaker liable if a patron insisted on wearing a shoe two sizes too small and damaged her feet. They noted an earlier case, in which a do-it-yourselfer bought ready-mixed cement. While smoothing out freshly-poured cement, he received burns from its caustic chemicals. Professionals know there is lime in cement, said the court. It went on to say that the caustic properties of lime have been known for centuries. Therefore, there was no duty to warn of it. After considering these and several other cases, the court concluded that people who use cologne don't know it's flammable.

This reasoning is faulty when the cement case is stacked next to it. If it's common knowledge that cement has lime as an ingredient, and that lime burns, then how is it outside the common realm that cologne contains alcohol and it burns? *Webster's New International Dictionary* defines "cologne" as "A perfumed liquid composed of alcohol… " The *Encyclopedia Americana* describes *Eau de Cologne,* as "a fragrant water… manufactured by adding to distilled alcohol a few aromatic oils… the general process of manufacture is known." *Webster's New Collegiate Dictionary* defines "alcohol" as "a colorless volatile flammable liquid." The court's reasoning stinks. It ignores the very authorities it cites. Moreover, it discards common sense. The court rewarded stupidity.

In this poorly-reasoned appellate opinion, came the language that spirited manufacturers to supply warning labels everywhere. In balancing the cost of alerting users with the danger of not warning them, the court proclaimed:

> [T]he cost of giving an adequate warning is usually so minimal, amounting only to the expense of adding some more printing to a label, that this balancing process will almost always weigh in favor of an obligation to warn of latent dangers…

This fanciful piece of information ignorantly minimized the cost of changing labels on every item in the country that contained enough alcohol to make it flammable. While a company the size of *Fabergé* could afford it, it would be expensive. Changing one word on a business card doubled the cost on my last set. Imagine what it cost to rework the label of every product affected by the decision. This caught *Fabergé* and every other manufacturer in the country.

A single decision about warnings cost manufacturers and suppliers millions and millions of dollars. Of course, since it was applied evenly across the board against all manufacturers, they all raised their prices for the retooling without losing any competitiveness. So, who paid for all those millions of dollars? The consumers.

The *Fabergé* decision caused many alert notices to be slapped on hair sprays and colognes. But it was done for a good reason, according to the judge. He wanted consumers warned of impending hidden dangers. If it stopped one accident, so the argument goes, it's worth all those millions.

Don't be misled into thinking that these warnings are prominently displayed on the bottles. Producers want you to purchase their products. Therefore, anything that alarms a potential customer is cloaked. Each of the warning notices described earlier is either buried in the body of the directions or it's so integrated into the label that casual readers would ignore it. They're not on the bottles to give notice, they're there because the courts said that it was cheap to put them on so you better do it.

Apparently, the court wanted to hold *Fabergé* liable, and it did. Before the court was a young girl who had been injured and a deep-pocketed defendant. Lawyers often say that good facts make bad law. This is a glaring example of it. Emotionally, most people root for an injured girl to overcome the rich corporation, even when the company was right and the young lady was wrong. Logically, the adolescent should have been held accountable for her foolish participation in scenting the candle. Emotions obviously won the battle; the opinion the judge wrote disregarded common sense.

Bowser Bit Me

The question arises whether these labels effectively shield anyone from liability. The answer is yes, but with some qualifications. Product Liability has three different aspects:

A well-designed product can be poorly constructed, and the defect makes it dangerous. Also, the item can be properly manufactured, but the design of it is dangerous. No amount of warning would protect a maker of either of these goods. These items shouldn't be marketed to anyone. Finally, the item might have hidden properties that need to be identified to protect the user from harm. It's this category where the labels protect manufacturers and all other defendants.

Sometimes the warnings hoisted a proper shield. Since Product Liability is a complex area of the law, these cases may help explain it:

Posting "bad dog" signs around a fenced business area gave sufficient notice to an employee that the guard dogs were afoot. Likewise, a "Beware of the Dog" sign gave notice to a 10-year-old boy to stay away.

A little more depth is required for the next dog cases because the warnings weren't as clearly given. A truck driver was dispatched to an aquarium supply company located on the East Coast. It was his first time there. While inside the office, the driver got impatient waiting for someone to help him. He saw two doors. The court's opinion described a picture.

Posted on the door to the warehouse was a sign with a drawing of a bulldog with its mouth wide open as it sneeringly displayed a grid of sharp, large canines. The sign boldly proclaimed "TRESPASSERS WILL BE EATEN."

On the other door was a sign depicting a bulldog wearing a guard's hat. It said, "GUARD DOG ON DUTY." Disbelieving the signs, the driver knocked on the warehouse door and heard muffled voices inside. He opened the door and breached the barrier. As he entered, several employees shouted, "Get out! There's a dog in here." Shortly after the warning, a 100-pound German shepherd pounced and chomped on the driver's left hand.

The trucker filed the inevitable lawsuit. In litigation, he learned that if a person of normal intelligence in his position would have understood the danger, the warning is effective. The court held that "TRESPASSERS WILL BE EATEN" is a serious message, despite its comical style. The truck driver assumed the risk of being attacked when he entered the warehouse.

Another dog case involved a licensed veterinarian with many years experience. He examined a woman's dog that was brought in for neutering. She hoped the operation would "mellow" the dog. When the vet reached down, the dog snapped at his arm. The vet asked its owner, "When were you going to tell me the dog might bite, after he has my arm?" He then handed her a muzzle to put on the dog. The vet saw her struggle before finally securing the device on the dog's snout.

The vet performed a pre-neutering examination on a table, and then placed the dog back on the floor. In a stroke of brilliance, the vet apparently disregarded the earlier snapping event and the difficulty the owner had installing the muzzle. He must have thought that he had control of the animal. When he removed the muzzle, the dog bit him several times. The vet bit back by suing the owner for her dog's unsavory deportment. The court held that the vet had plenty of notice of the dog's aggressiveness, and was entitled to nothing in his law-suit.

These cases teach us that warnings can be verbal, written, or circumstantial. Courts apply common sense in most of the cases, and hold for the dog owners if a warning precedes an attack. In other words, reckless plaintiffs lose. If a person is warned and he ignores the warning, he assumes the risk.

To Boldly Go Where No Warnings Have Gone Before

Sometimes, people must warn others. Other times there isn't any need. The following describes a case where a warning would have been effective, but the doctor refused to give it. A physician dated a nurse and the couple ultimately had sexual relations.

At the time of their fornication, the doctor allegedly knew that his genital herpes was active. In describing the disease, the court said it was a contagious, painful, and incurable malady that is spread by having sex. The nurse apparently caught the disease from the silent doctor.

His reason for silence is fairly obvious, and tremendously selfish. He wanted to score. A venereal disease alert could well have thwarted his quest. The court called the doctor's conduct "extreme and outrageous" for not giving notice of the disease. She won her suit, but would have lost if she had been warned of the danger.

In another case, a fellow bought a *Yamaha* motorcycle. While riding it, he collided with an automobile and injured his left leg. The motorcyclist sued, claiming that the motorcycle wasn't "crashworthy" and that he wasn't warned that 90 percent of all serious non-fatal injuries in motorcycle collisions involved the lower part of the rider's body. The biker asserted that he should have been warned.

The court cited the *Fabergé* case and said that "the duty of the manufacturer to warn applies only to inherent and hidden dangers—latent dangers not readily apparent to the consumer... But a seller is not required to warn with respect to products... when the danger, is generally known and recognized."

It's contradictory logic. Since the court ruled that reasonable people don't know that cologne contains alcohol, or that alcohol burns, *Fabergé* is liable. But, since another court ruled that everyone knows motorcycles break legs, *Yamaha* isn't.

Discrepancies like this drive lawyers crazy. They must guess what will pop out next from the judicial jack-in-the-box. Assume a client who owns a prophylactic company went to an attorney and asked, "Should I put a warning label on this product?" The attorney isn't being evasive when he says, "Maybe."

Reconsider the preceding cases that force the lawyer into the indefinite answer. The *Yamaha* court said that everyone who rides motorcycles knows how dangerous they are. Warnings are unnecessary if everyone knows about a danger. With all of the publicity about AIDS and venereal disease, most Americans understand that sexual intercourse can spread viruses. They've also heard that condoms help curb the transmission, but aren't foolproof.

On the other hand, courts from the same jurisdiction proclaimed that reasonable people don't know that alcohol is the main ingredient of cologne, and that the average person doesn't know alcohol is flammable. At the same time, the courts say that everyone who uses cement knows it contains lime, and that lime is caustic.

Judicial opinions often weigh upon what was for breakfast, or if there is an upcoming election, or how attractive a litigant is to a judge. This can lead to arbitrary results and incongruity.

Since decisions are influenced by personal motives as well as by justice, lawyers must speculate what direction the courts might turn next. This isn't all bad for the lawyers. The uncertainty in a field of the law translates into lots of legal work.

In the case of the client's condoms, the attorney decides it is better to err on the side of safety. Therefore, he advises that it would be best to apply a warning label that covers every known danger about the product. Because of the meeting, the client decides to paste multiple warnings on the label:

Condoms are not bullet proof. Severe stretching may cause condoms to fail; never use the wrong size. Always install this product *before* using it; if difficulty is experienced during installation, review page 2, paragraphs 7-9 of the instruction pamphlet. WARNING: This product is not 100 percent effective in preventing pregnancies or sexually transmitted diseases.

As an afterthought, the client inserts, "This product is for topical use and is not to be taken orally." One must wonder what suits would lurk for the unfortunate condom maker who affixed this confusing double entendre on the label. While it is prudent to warn the public of latent dangers, the notice must be clear and unequivocal.

As an example of an ambiguous warning, is the bottle of *Brut* Splash-On Lotion that started this chapter. On the container, it cautions about flammability. However, above the warning, in larger type, it says:

Splash-On Brut... after shave, after shower, after anything!

That little slogan is a registered trademark of *Fabergé*. It could spell trouble for them because it sends a double message, just like the condom afterthought warning. While people are warned that the product is flammable, they are also told that it can be splashed on after anything.

Considering what the court said in the previous *Fabergé* case, it could mean trouble for the manufacturer. If someone splashed it on while lighting a candle, a fireplace, or a welding torch, they might win because they were deceived about the product's hidden volatility. I guess some companies need to be sued every few years to remember any lessons of the past. Lawyers can advise their clients, but their clients—especially corporations—often don't listen.

If One Is Good, How About 29?

Since it is better to warn, than to omit notice, the manufacturers have gone absolutely nuts. Earlier in the chapter, we discussed several bottles of hair spray that were loaded with warnings. For curiosity, check some products around the house for an overabundance of warnings.

A 16-ounce *Stanley* Professional Hammer sports the following ornament: "Never strike this hammer... against... [a] hardened nail... " One might wonder of what use is a hammer that can't strike a nail. The entire warning is:

WARNING — PROTECT YOUR EYES — WEAR SAFETY GOGGLES This hammer is intended only for driving and pulling common and finish nails. Never strike this hammer with or against another striking tool, hardened nail, chisel, or any hard object. Chipping can occur, possibly resulting in eye injury, blindness, or other bodily injury to the user or bystander.

The *Stanley* lawyers tried covering all bases. They have seen juries give plaintiffs grand-slam home runs before, and they want to keep the score down. They not only try to tell what it is intended to be used as, but also warn of what the danger is, and who could get hurt. Even these zealous advocates have fallen prey to a warning label error. A careful reading leads one to assume that this hammer in not intended for box nails, annular ring nails, roofing nails, casing nails, common brads, or duplex head nails.

Checking with a housing contractor with decades of experience, I learned that if a hammer is a competent instrument for common and finish nails, it should be adequate for all the others in the preceding paragraph. Even a lay person could compare a brad and a finish nail and conclude they are similar. Common sense dictates that if it can pound finishing nails, it can pound brads just as safely. The contractor confirmed this.

Now, *Stanley* faces another dilemma. Did they try to go so far with the warning that they violated consumer protection statutes? It could be construed that a person who took this warning seriously would purchase different hammers for those other types of nails. I assume that this would never happen. The reason is that almost nobody reads the warning labels because there are so many of them. And even if they do look at them, the alert notices aren't taken seriously. We're so over-warned that we're numb. The warnings have little or no credibility.

However, just in case they were trying to trick the public into purchasing needless tools, I checked ten different *Stanley* claw hammers at a hardware store. All of them contained the same warning. Apparently none of them were suitable for hitting brads. No foul—probably. But what about a tack hammer? Maybe that's what they recommend for brads. But aren't tack hammers just for tacks?

To help the *Stanley* attorneys out of their dilemma, I have graciously provided them with a list that should meet judicial muster.

1. Do not use this tool while under the influence of drugs or alcohol;
2. Keep fingers away from the striking area;
3. Do not hold nail while someone else hammers it;
4. Do not hit anyone with a hammer—It is not a toy;
5. Keep out of reach of children;
6. Do not use this hammer to pop a pimple;
7. Do not hold hammer while engaged in a domestic struggle.

Checking other tools, I noticed that some drill bits and table-saw blades are dangerous. Warnings alert potential users to always wear eye protection that complies with current ANSI Standard 87.1. Being curious, I checked safety goggles and found that about half the models stocked met the guidelines. The type of notice on the drill bits is the worst of all worlds for a consumer. It warns of danger unless ANSI 87.1 is complied with, yet the average person has no idea what that means. It's designed to protect the manufacturer of the drill bit if someone gets blinded using it and their goggles weren't certified by ANSI. It's almost useless to the consumer, but it could shield the manufacturer in a lawsuit.

Next, came my inspection of ladders. A 6-foot step ladder came with no fewer than 29 separate warnings about ladder safety pasted on its frame. These warnings aren't there to alert the public. There are too many to read and retain. They're strictly to cover the posterior of the manufacturer.

A contractor told me of a step ladder he recently purchased which had at least 16 warnings on labels attached to it. What he also advised was to stick with wooden ladders. While most

everyone realizes that an aluminum ladder might cause elec-
trocution in a storm, something they might overlook is an
equally real hazard.

Aluminum fatigues. But it might not be apparent from a
visual inspection that a rung is dangerous. If a rung gives way
while a person is standing on it, it breaks, and the remaining
metal edges slash the person falling through the ladder. Ground
impact injuries are often small compared to the carving done
by the metal ladder's jagged teeth.

With wood, one can effectively inspect the rungs. Further,
should someone fall through a wooden one, the rung cuts are
minimized. The average person would be ignorant of this
danger. However, none of the aluminum ladders I investigated warned that they were more dangerous than wooden
ones. The reason is clear. They want to sell their product. The
labels are for them, not for the buyer. In reality, anyone knows
that climbing any ladder is dangerous. Anyone who spends
enough time off the ground will eventually have an accident.
No amount of warnings will stop this.

To my wonder, shovels, rakes, and hoes bore no warnings.
Even pitchforks with menacing tangs were exempted from the
notices. I expected to read, "WARNING: Do not use for
eating spaghetti.

Show Your Health Hazards

Cautionary labels bombard us to boredom. An ordinary
bottle of aspirin contains multiple precautions. Even if the
minuscule writing on it were readable, comprehension is unlikely when someone feels lousy.

When drugs are considered, some different rules apply.
Producers of diethylstilbestrol (DES) marketed a drug that
was supposed to prevent pregnant women from miscarrying
the fetus. Unfortunately, the drug reportedly caused injury to

some of the babies that it saved. Courts gave the drug companies a little extra protection from the label mania.

They reasoned that doctors need to be warned by the manufacturer of known dangers at the time (as opposed to hazards learned later). Apparently, only doctors are bright enough to understand complex warnings. Then, it is incumbent upon the physicians to warn their respective patients. That's why regular aspirin might sport over 200 words of precaution, and aspirin that also contains codeine, a prescription drug, says only: "Take as needed for pain."

Extra protection is given drug companies so they will bound forward into new areas of research. Lawsuits cripple them already, according to the courts and the companies. While this bit of logic seems out of place when considering huge corporations that rake in boxcars of profit, some of these cases show what happens when lawsuits reign and reason dies.

Merrell Dow Pharmaceuticals pulled *Bendectin* from the market in 1983. At the time, it was the only anti-nausea drug available for pregnant women. The reason was that insurance costs for the drug prohibited its production. Insurance rates are a direct reflection of litigation. Today, pregnant women have little relief from nausea because so many lawsuits were filed.

To counter the removal of the drug, some physicians are bootlegging a look-alike. Since there is no approved anti-nausea drug available, many recommend over-the-counter remedies such as Unisom, Dramamine, or Bonine. So, some pregnant women get relief from morning sickness, but it is not without risk.

This time, however, most of the risk is borne by the helpful doctor. Unisom is packaged with a warning against using it during pregnancy. The reason for the warning, of course, is to protect the manufacturer. Many physicians would rate the remedy as relatively risk-free. But just wait for one of these mothers to deliver a child with a malady. Then watch the lawyers chomp into the doctor who "recklessly disregarded" the manufacturer's warning. And this will happen. About 3 percent of all children suffer from congenital abnormalities whether their mother took medication or not. It will happen; the only question is when.

Isn't it sad that our system of "dialing for dollars" will make a martyr of some doctors who had the compassion to ignore silly warnings to comfort their patients. Aren't these the type of doctors we want? Isn't it about time we let physicians heal the afflicted instead of covering their rear from wolves that won't heel?

If pregnant women think our courts will rescue them from the lack of drugs for anti-nausea, they need to think again. There is little empathy coming from the bench; not many judges in America have had morning sickness.

The U.S. Supreme court slammed the door on *Bendectin* in June of 1993. The Court announced that despite the fact that 30 credible studies involving 130,000 humans have failed to demonstrate that *Bendectin* is capable of causing malformations in fetuses, plaintiffs can still sue the manufacturer. All they need to do is locate an expert witness who can testify about scientific knowledge that will assist courts in understanding *possible* adverse side-effects of the drug. It seems that any kind of scientist can testify as an expert, even if the theory offered flies in the face of generally-accepted scientific opinion.

The situation is this: Women often suffer morning sickness when pregnant; there are drugs to relieve this symptom that the medical community accepts as relatively safe, but to avoid lawsuits the makers refuse to sell the remedies. Therefore, pregnant women will suffer morning sickness because there is no "legally" acceptable relief. In sealing expecting mothers' fate to nausea, the Court made an astounding statement:

It is true that open debate is an essential part of both legal and scientific analyses. Yet there are important differences between the quest for truth in the courtroom and the quest for truth in the laboratory. Scientific conclusions are subject to perpetual revision. Law, on the other hand, must resolve disputes finally and quickly.

Justice Blackmun, the author of the opinion, apparently thinks that courts are fast-acting and that they act with finality. That is truly amazing. First, the *Bendectin* opinion overruled a standard of assessing whether an expert was qualified to give an opinion that had stood for 70 years. Nothing is final when precedents of that age are subject to fall.

Our courts are in crisis with overcrowded calendars that drag the judicial works. An assertion about swift justice ignores this. *Bendectin* has been off the market for ten years, yet the courts are still deciding who can and who can't testify in the cases. Courts don't have cheetah-like quickness; their plodding efforts more resemble the movements of a tree sloth. Maybe the Justice had his tongue firmly planted in his cheek when he wrote the prose. Yet, the opinion astonishingly reaffirms the goal of courts: to mete out swift and certain justice, "...reaching a quick, final, and binding legal judgment..."

Perhaps it will take a score of years to try this case; that's judicial "quickness."

In another case, a new discovery of a vaccine for flu made prevention of an epidemic possible. The drug companies couldn't afford the legal risk of mass inoculations. The government had to assume liability before the shots were given.

Another vaccine cost 11 cents in 1982. Four years later, the same vaccine jumped to over 11 *dollars*, a one-hundredfold increase. Insurance reserves, lawsuits, and greed accounted for the surge.

A patient who suffered from a side effect of *Mutamycin* claimed lack of warning by the manufacturer. When the drug was made, it was known that the same side effect hampered about 4 percent of recipients of the drugs. The court protected the drug manufacturers, reasoning that doctors get enough warning about any drug if the statement is contained in the *Physician's Desk Reference*.

Liability slid over to the treating doctor. It's their duty to tell a patient of side effects, warnings, and the like. So, the courts reduced drug maker's exposure to encourage them to develop new products. However, by shifting the burden to the physician for warning of the drugs, the courts have all but guaranteed the new drugs won't be prescribed. Doctors aren't stupid. Why should they stick out their necks on new products when the drug companies are immune? Our courts have done it again.

A generic bottle of aspirin marketed by *Western Family* contains 100 tablets of 325 milligram doses of the drug. On the back of the bottle is a warning measuring 1-1/2" x 5/8" containing over 240 words.

Although slightly near-sighted, I have excellent vision for close work and require no lenses for reading. However, in less than a square inch, the manufacturer packed nearly a full page of the book you have in your hands. To show you how tiny this is, the actual warning is reproduced. While I could read the words, it would give me a terrible headache and eyestrain. It should have said, WARNING: Do not attempt to read this label without taking two aspirin.

WARNINGS: Children and teenagers should not use this medicine for chicken pox or flu symptoms before a doctor is consulted about Reye Syndrome, a rare but serious illness reported to be associated with aspirin. Do not take the product for more than 10 days for adults and not more than 5 days for children. If fever persists for more than 3 days (72 hours), or recurs, or if symptoms persist or if new ones occur, consult your doctor. Stop taking this product if ringing in the ears or other symptoms occur. As with any drug, if you are pregnant or nursing a baby, seek the advice of a health professional before using this product. IT IS ESPECIALLY IMPORTANT NOT TO USE ASPIRIN DURING THE LAST THREE MONTHS OF PREGNANCY UNLESS SPECIFICALLY DIRECTED TO DO SO BY A DOCTOR BECAUSE IT MAY CAUSE PROBLEMS IN THE UNBORN CHILD OR COMPLICATIONS DURING DELIVERY. Keep this and all drugs out of the reach of children. In case of accidental overdose, seek professional assistance or contact a poison control center immediately.
Do not take this product if you have ulcers or are presently taking a prescription drug for anticoagulation (thinning the blood), diabetes, gout, or arthritis except under the advice and supervision of a doctor. Do not take this product if you are allergic to aspirin or if you have asthma except under the advice and supervision of a doctor.
CAUTION: If seal under cap is missing or torn, do not use this product.

Here is the complete warning label in easier-to-read type:

WARNINGS: Children and teenagers should not use this medicine for chicken pox or flu symptoms before a doctor is consulted about Reye Syndrome, a rare but serious illness reported to be associated with aspirin. Do not take the product for more than 10 days for adults and not more than 5 days for children. If fever persists for more than 3 days (72 hours), or recurs, or if symptoms persist or if new ones occur, consult your doctor. Stop taking this product if ringing in the ears or other symptoms occur. As with any drug, if you are pregnant or nursing a baby, seek the advice of a health professional before using this product. IT IS ESPECIALLY IMPORTANT NOT TO USE ASPIRIN DURING THE LAST THREE MONTHS OF PREGNANCY UNLESS SPECIFICALLY DIRECTED TO DO SO BY A DOCTOR BECAUSE IT MAY CAUSE PROBLEMS IN THE UNBORN CHILD OR COMPLICATIONS DURING DELIVERY. Keep this and all drugs out of the reach of children. In case of accidental overdose, seek professional assistance or contact a poison control center immediately.
Do not take this product if you have ulcers or are presently taking a prescription drug for anticoagulation (thinning the blood), diabetes, gout, or arthritis except under the advice and supervision of a doctor. Do not take this product if you are allergic to aspirin or if you have

asthma except under the advice and supervision of a doctor.

CAUTION: If seal under cap is missing or torn, do not use this product.

Give and Take

In the following case, a manufacturer warded off a lawsuit because of labels it applied to caution users of its go-cart: When a boy drove one on the public highway, he took along his 6-year-old brother for a ride. At an intersection, a car struck the go-cart, killing the go-cart driver.

His parents went to court, claiming the cart to be defective because it was so low to the ground it was nearly invisible to most vehicles on the street. They claimed that the cart needed a pole strutting a flag protruding from it to give it better visibility.

As stated earlier, the manufacturer had wisely affixed two separate labels that stated in clear terms that the cart was not to be used on public streets. The warnings saved the manufacturer, but not the boy.

Another company decided to affix warning labels to its cement about the caustic properties of lime. It put the labels on most bags, but one customer purchased a bag with no warnings affixed to it. Ignorant and unwarned, he lay in the cement and burned himself. The court said that if you warn one, you better warn all. They found the company liable for failure to warn by omitting the label.

A ruling like this has troublesome implications. Before a manufacturer labeled cement as dangerous, consumers were expected to know its properties. Once a warning is attached, it better remain on all of the packages. That means whatever warnings are given today, dare not be removed—ever. And new warnings will be added to the list to suit the courts. If this continues, the warnings will become the dominant portion of all product-packaging.

The warnings are everywhere. We hear that cigarettes cause low birth weight in babies, hardening of the arteries, lung cancer, heart disease, and sundry other problems. The cover of a *2 Live Crew* album, the Florida rap group famous for crassness, warns that explicit language is used. Beer bottles warn of dangers of consuming alcohol when pregnant or while driving a vehicle. A *Lobo Paramilitary Christmas Special* comic book bears the following alert:

> WARNING: Contains Bad Taste In The Form Of Ultra-Violence, Icon-Bashing, And "The Finger." More Offensive Than Christmas Usually Is.

At least *DC Comics* had the sense to parody the warning label idiocy. Some labels tell us not to drink shoe polish, while others urge us not to clean contact lenses with ammonia. The public is taken for suckers and fools. No one could take the deluge of cautionary notices seriously.

Looking through a *Honda Accord* Owner's manual, I discovered the following alerts on page two.

⚠DANGER indicates severe personal injury or death will result if instructions are not followed.

♨WARNING indicates a strong possibility of severe personal injury or death if instructions are not followed.

CAUTION: means hazards or unsafe practices which could cause minor personal injury or product or property damage.

In a manual that contains only 132 pages is one DANGER alert with the triangle and exclamation point. This is supplemented by at least 50 WARNING hands and 39 CAUTION notices. Included in these important messages is a warning not to drive with the glove box open. Another proclaims that gasoline is flammable. One even says that if hands are stuck out windows that an injury could result. It would take a good deal of effort to commit all 90 alerts to memory.

One particularly useless notice cautions that when the engine kills or if the power steering unit fails, the car can still be steered. "However, much greater effort will be required, particularly in sharp turns at low speed." In case this caution is forgotten when attempting to memorize the other 89, just turn to page 87 of the manual. That would be a treat while trying to steer a car that rounds corners like a Mack truck as it crashes down a mountain road.

There is only one purpose for all this nonsense. It's to satisfy the court that a warning was given. With 90 warnings, nobody cares about any of them. The notices are absurd, but, our vigilant courts are happy.

The Never-Ending Warning

We are saturated with warnings. One day we hear about the dangers of ozone depletion. On another, we learn that exposure to sunlight might give us cancer. Electricity causes all manor of malaise according to some reports. *Alar* sprayed on apples causes cancer, proclaim others. Red meat consumption causes massive artery damage declare some experts. If meat is undercooked, you might suffer from E. coli poisoning. However, if the same meat is overcooked, then it's claimed to cause cancer. Formaldehyde might also be carcinogenic. If we listened to all the warnings, we wouldn't eat fruit or meat. We'd stay inside all day, but avoid our clothes, carpets, walls, and toothpaste that contained formaldehyde. And of course, we'd have our electrical service disconnected.

Most of these warnings were given because experiments with laboratory animals showed the critters developed health problems when overexposed or underexposed to various stimuli. Upon learning of potential health risks, the scientific community sent out warning messages that frightened the public. Often, these tests were based upon such distorted circumstances that there was no relation to reality. Who really cares if a laboratory rat eats a bushel of beans and gasses itself to death? Maybe we should heed the advice of Notre Dame football coach, Lou Holtz, who considered the problem and said, "We don't need more lab tests, what we need are healthier rats."

Some warnings should be given. We need traffic lights at busy intersections and stop signs at blind corners. But is it wise to speculate prematurely, and alarmingly so, that electricity might make us sick? To use warnings as a public service makes sense. To abuse them for litigation defense is irresponsible.

An example of a mandated warning appeared in the *LA Times*. Mushroom gathering is a common practice in the Commonwealth of Independent States. Unfortunately, several varieties of harmless mushrooms have mutated or otherwise changed into deadly toadstools. Radioactivity is suspected, but scientists are baffled at what caused the transformation. Hundreds of cases of poisoning were reported and at least 60 Russian and Ukrainian citizens have died of the toxin. Television news broadcast an unprecedented warning. Here is a case where the public needed to know. It was right out of the script of the "B" science fiction thriller-spoof, *Attack of the Killer Tomatoes*. A previously harmless item turned into a deadly menace.

Then, consider the missing warnings that started this chapter. Imagine the foolish adolescent Getcha Allen grabbing a bottle of *Tigress Cologne* off the shelf gleefully ready to flood the candle with scent. Just before making the bomb, she stops, reads a label, and thinks, *This is flammable. I better not do it.* It's probably out of the question. How effective would the label have been under those circumstances? However, a similar label now protects *Fabergé* from irresponsible users.

Everything is in line for the warning-label mania. Food is probably next. My investigation revealed that table sugar is devoid of warning labels. One might think that with so many diabetics in this country that an alert notice would go on beet and cane products. It would be incorrect to presume that. Sugar appears to be a protected item. Everyone in the country must know that it aggravates diabetes.

Oddly, though, the *Coca-Cola Company* apparently doesn't want to advertise sugar content in its drinks. It sweetens *Coke* and *Sprite* with "HIGH FRUCTOSE CORN SYRUP AND/OR SUCROSE." This is a cloaking device. "Fructose" and "Sucrose" *are* both sugars. If this is a marketing ploy to disguise the sweetener, it might backfire in a failure-to-warn case by some poor soul who unwittingly consumed sugar in *Coca Cola* and went into a diabetic coma.

The clutter of all the notices actually increases the danger to the public. Imagine driving down a street where amber lights flash alerting you of a dip in the road. You drive a few feet and notice a minor dip, but nothing traumatic. One block later, you see flashing blue lights and slow down only to discover that a police officer left his light rack on while he stopped for a donut. A block later is another amber flasher for a dip. You slow, but never notice a dip in the road. A block farther, an amber light blinks around a sign that says: "WARNING BRIDGE OUT AHEAD." The sign goes unread. It's ignored because nobody cares about another dip in the road.

Two blocks later, you slam the brake pedal to the floorboard, but it's too late. The car skids through a barricade and falls from the broken bridge into the river.

Under those facts, you should sue the court. Unfortunately, we have a doctrine of judicial immunity, which means you can't usually sue a judge for deciding a case. This should be the exception. It's the courts' idiotic rulings that have led us to warning-label saturation.

Isn't this fun—No, don't look for the end of this warning mania quite yet. I'm warning you.

CHAPTER 9

Solutions

The previous eight chapters of *Crisis In Our Courts* have identified many—certainly not all—of the flaws in our judicial system. The following remedies are offered to improve our system so that ants and gi-ants are treated equally under the law, and with the hope we will soon return to juries "of the people."

"Juries," said Mr. Bumble, grasping his cane tightly, as was his wont when working into a passion: "juries is ineddicated, vulgar, grovelling wretches."

When Charles Dickens wrote the preceding passage in *Oliver Twist*, he was satirizing boarding schools. In America, somebody must have missed the humor and taken Charlie at face value. When the mistake was made, lawyers and judges stole the rights of average citizens to be represented on juries.

Solution 1
Preserve Jury Trials

They're hated, they're loved. Despised and cherished. They're the cornerstone of justice and the foothold of bigotry.

Juries enjoy a long history in the United States. When their verdicts appear correct, they're the apex of the legal system. Should they render a flawed decision, they're scorned and a woeful blemish for us to bear.

Juries often blow it and render bad verdicts. The $10 billion award in the *Texaco* case is an example of a terrible jury verdict. Whether *Pennzoil* should have won anything is debatable, but the win they got was billions of dollars more than anybody could have dreamed possible. This is but one of thousands of horrible jury verdicts.

In addition to being lambasted for awarding many idiotic verdicts, juries are criticized for being too unsophisticated to deal with the complexities of lawsuits. Further, the additional expense of jury trials is frequently cited as a reason to abolish them. Many critics want juries totally eliminated. They argue that since as few as 8 percent of our cases are decided by juries, they are unnecessary dinosaurs. Noted jurist, Jerome Frank, criticized juries for misapplying law they can't grasp to facts they confuse beyond recognition. Former Supreme Court Chief Justice Warren Burger views civil jury trials as needless.

One argument is that since juries are rarely used we should forfeit our right to them. This is specious and asinine. As stated earlier in the book, 90 percent of all criminal trials are settled by guilty pleas. Since only 10 percent of criminal matters go to trial, opponents of jury trials might also argue to ban all criminal trials as needless procedures.

More compelling from supporters of jury trials is the argument that terror can be wrought upon people by a government that ignores the conscience of the common people. Aldof Hitler's judges were all accountable for their decisions, not to the people, but to *der Führer*. Destruction and genocide might have been spared the world if Nazi Germany had allowed jury trials.

We live in a society where a trial by jury is taken for granted as an absolute right. The foundation for the right to a trial by jury comes from the highest authority in American jurisprudence, the Constitution. If critics want to discard jury trials like yesterday's newspapers, they must amend the Constitution, which is totally unrealistic. However, judges and lawyers have effectively circumvented the Constitution and banned the man on the street from participating on juries. We must stubbornly adhere to the right to trial by jury, and be suspicious of anyone who wants to dilute that right.

Solution 2
Respect Juror Privacy – Restrict Voir Dire

When a jury summons arrives, the recipient loses his privacy. As discussed earlier, wealthy and powerful litigants screen potential jurors for biases. The rich hire private detectives and pry into the affairs of potential jurors. The government uses "official" detectives to snoop by doing such things as pulling criminal-record files to determine the desirability of jurors. This is patently unfair to parties with less money or power who can't afford such luxuries. But worse, it invades jurors' privacy. There is no need to know that a potential juror attends a church or a synagogue, is married or single, lives in a tenement or a mansion. All we need to know is whether they can read and write the English language and if they are eligible to vote in elections. If they are qualified to vote for our president, they're qualified to vote on a jury.

The reason that American jurors are subjected to such invasion of their privacy rests primarily upon a single case. United States Supreme Court Chief Justice John Marshall invented a legal game at the beginning of the nineteenth century when a former vice president faced treason charges. The events were highly publicized, and many people had already formed opinions of his guilt or innocence. Marshall feared that randomly-selected jurors would convict Aaron Burr without regard to the evidence. To ferret out these horrid jurors, the Chief Justice allowed every juror to be subjected to voir dire (quizzing the jurors).

Each juror was questioned by counsel as the lawyers tried to uncover biases of prospective jurors. Those considered prejudiced were discarded from the jury pool. Whether Marshall intended to rig the trial is unknown, but questioning jurors for bias resulted in a jury that favored Burr. Our notorious vice president who allegedly collaborated with the British to sever the United States was acquitted by a jury laden with sympathizers.

Two centuries later, our courts still use voir dire in search of the "ineddicated, vulgar, grovelling wretches" that infest our jury pools. Every person who is summoned for jury duty is presumed to be too prejudiced to give a fair hearing of the evidence. Judges and lawyers assume that jurors are ignorant, prejudiced, and wretched. That's why we continue playing Justice John Marshall's game in the courtroom, so the attorneys can prove that most jurors are bigots. Citizens need to vehemently resist this unwarranted government intrusion into their lives.

I asked several competent trial attorneys where the voir dire process originated. Not one of them knew. They all accepted it as the traditional approach to jury selection, and each was surprised that it wasn't used in England or Canada. None of them thought that the system was improper and all defended it.

I doubt that many lawyers view themselves as jury maulers or voyeurs. They perceive voir dire as a tool to use while zealously representing their clients. Further, they see nothing wrong because centuries of tradition supports jury-rigging.

American jurors line up for the abuse like so many sheep. Jury members accept the shearing because it's always been this way; they don't realize that they can resist it. Awed by marble corridors, oak walls, and distinguished judges, jurors crumble to the power of the court.

In the courtroom, the jurors hang on every word of the learned judge, and blindly accept wisdom that comes from the bench. When the judge says that the attorneys are going to ask some personal questions, and that it is proper for them to do so, the jurors believe it.

So, the sheep comply with the prying into even the most intimate aspects of their lives. Jurors are questioned about sex, money, and sundry matters that they wouldn't consider discussing with anyone, including their spouses.

Attorneys claim to be asking the questions in search of a "fair and impartial" panel. That's bunk. They're busy stacking the jury to be prejudiced toward their client. When judges allow lawyers to ask these embarrassing questions, they're sanctioning voyeurism. Juror's privacy rights shouldn't be crushed because they were summoned to court.

The argument in support of lawyer-screening of jury members is to acquire a "fair and impartial" jury. As discussed earlier in the book, lawyers don't want fair jurors, they want prejudiced ones. Beyond that, the right of litigants to have "fair trials" must be balanced against the right of "juror privacy" and I submit that the scale weighs far more heavily for citizen's rights than for individual litigants.

There is no justification for intrusive voir dire except to allow lawyers better control of the courtroom. Citizens will have more say in courts if they can participate without being spied upon by lawyers and litigants. Voir dire should be restricted to only the most obvious questions. I submit that the only questions that need be asked of any jurors are:

1. Are you related to any parties, lawyers, or witnesses in this case?
2. Do you know any parties, attorneys, or witnesses involved with this case?
3. Have you made up your mind who should prevail in this case?
4. Will you base your verdict on statements made outside the courtroom that are not in evidence?
5. Will you let bias or prejudice affect your decision?

Should the jurors answer "no" to all the questions, then they are accepted on the panel. If the answer to any of these questions is "yes," then, and only then, should attorneys be allowed limited voir dire to attempt to expose unreasonable bias. If counsel proves the juror can't be fair, that juror is rejected.

Solution 3
Show Jurors Some Respect—
Abolish Peremptory Challenges

While pretending to look for impartial members, the lawyers are playing a cunning and roguish game during voir dire. They listen to responses and watch body language for tips about which way a juror might vote. Those who appear to be against them are discarded. There is no search for a "fair and impartial" juror, but for biased ones, pre-disposed in their client's direction.

Sometimes, legal advocates go overboard. Brazen lawyers have pulled every black person—every white person—every female—every male from panels. When lawyers are bold enough to blatantly do this, they get caught. The Supreme Court says it's illegal to do it. So do statutes. But, most attorneys understand the rules and bend them as far as possible. Therefore, they deceptively claim to be removing panelists for reasons other than race, creed, age, or sex, giving the illusion that the bump was legal.

Citizens have been slapped for centuries by trial lawyers, and it's time they counter-punched. Every time a lawyer bumps a juror from a case, that attorney has effectually said: "You're a bigot. You can't make a fair decision." Allowing it to continue is shameful, tragic, and unjust. Lawyers should have this power ripped from their briefcases. Citizens shouldn't endure such trauma just so the legal advocates can rig a jury.

People are bumped from jury panels because of skin color, accent, ancestry, education, height, weight, and any number of discriminatory reasons that are absolutely forbidden outside the courtroom. A lawyer can wake up in the morning and say: "I don't think I want any old people on this jury." In the courtroom, every senior citizen on the panel will be rejected.

Ironically, Justice John Marshall started voir dire and supported the peremptory challenge. In the twentieth century, another Supreme Court Justice named Marshall condemned the practice. In a concurring opinion, Thurgood Marshall wrote:

> The inherent potential of peremptory challenges to distort the jury process by permitting the exclusion of jurors on racial grounds should ideally lead the Court to ban them entirely from the criminal justice system... [O]nly by banning peremptories entirely can such discrimination be ended.

I would take Marshall's statement further, by banning peremptory challenges in criminal *and* civil trials. Justice demands that jurors serve when called, despite sex, race, or creed. Lawyers should be forbidden from ejecting jurors on a whim.

The strongest argument for allowing peremptory challenges is that there might be someone on the jury who the lawyer or the litigant doesn't feel comfortable with, or worse there might be a bigot on the panel. While it's true that some buffoons will be allowed to serve under my proposal, think about how many totally qualified jurors are humiliated just to let the lawyers pick and choose. And even if a person reeking with prejudice gets on a jury, there will be other people on the panel to keep the biased ones in line. Talk about throwing out the baby with the bath water, with peremptory challenges we let lawyers chuck whole families, whole tribes, whole genders, whole generations. This judicially sanctioned discrimination should be flushed into the sewer.

Solution 4
A Survival Guide Until Change Comes

To understand how degrading the process of jury selection has become, imagine the attorneys asking judges similar questions. "Your honor, since you're only 4'8" and my client is 6'4", will her height affect your decision?" This could be followed by: "My client was the first black woman to move into your all-white neighborhood. Considering that, don't you think you'll abuse my client?" If the attorney wasn't slapped with contempt, he could well be threatened with it.

Since judges won't stand for it, neither should jurors. Imagine a marshal blocking the entrance of a polling place and quizzing voters about their feelings on abortion. If they answered incorrectly, ballots would be denied them. In addition, they would be publicly scorned and humiliated for having the wrong opinion. That's what voir dire does in jury selection.

We should return to the type of juries that Thomas Jefferson wanted preserved. Jurors should be *randomly* selected from a pool of people that accurately reflects the community.

To see how far away we have gone from a random selection of people, consider the jury selection that occurred during the second Rodney King beating trial. After acquittals on state charges, there was such an outcry that the feds did something unusual. They put the police on trial again. Our Constitution says: "... nor shall any person for the same offense to be twice put in jeopardy of life or limb..." This is the double jeopardy clause.

There's a catch-22 in this clause because courts can force defendants to run the state's gauntlet and then face federal charges. Our courts reason that two sovereigns govern the same territory. When someone commits a crime against both governments, then the federal and local authorities can each charge the person for the same act. Therefore, defendants can be held in jeopardy for the same offense and tried by both the state and then the federal authorities. Using this reasoning, the police who beat King faced two separate trials.

The *Associated Press* reported about the jury selection for the second trial. Each of the 380 potential jurors filled out a 55-page questionnaire to assist lawyers in preparing for the interrogation process in voir dire. That means the court expected at least 300 jurors to be too prejudiced to act fairly. Attorneys planned to interrogate jurors for a full month as they sought to uncover the bigots. It's flagrantly insulting to the American people. One defense attorney, Harland Braun, said:

> You may wind up with an all-white jury. Society needs a multi-racial jury to make them feel that the trial is fair. But I'm somewhat skeptical about that. African-American jurors may feel pressure from the community that will make them unfair.

When the jury was expected to be sequestered for two months, which means they'll live in a hotel, *incommunication*, a law school dean explained that will also bias the jury pool:

> With a sequestered jury, you tend to end up with an older jury, more retired people or unemployed people. That may give you an unrepresentative jury as to community attitudes.

If the experts and participants already know that it won't be a representative jury, why ask any of the invasive, demeaning, and humiliating questions of potential jurors? The answer is to shape the jury to be "unfair and predisposed." Justice deserves a random pick of twelve from a pool of jurors that's made up of a representative sample of the community. The jury selection process that occurred for this trial was expensive, time consuming, and flagrantly abusive to the potential jurors.

Citizens can stop this abuse from continuing. Following this chapter is a sample letter I prepared for you to send to your representative. It briefly states that you view the jury selection process as degrading, discriminatory, and improper.

If enough people send this message to Congress, the law will change. For the interim period, before the barbaric process ends, there is relief. If you happen to be called for jury duty, don't give in to the attorney's power. Yes, you should answer the questions the judge instructs you to, but when embarrassing questions come up, don't be afraid to say: "I don't want to answer that question." Should the judge order you to respond, do so, otherwise you could be found in contempt of court.

Should an attorney evict you from the panel, rise and face the judge. As respectfully as possible, ask the court: "Your honor, may I please have the name and address of the attorney who rejected me from the panel?"

The court will probably instruct the lawyer to give you a business card. The table is turned. You, the victim of the lawyer's discriminatory abuse, are now the intimidator. The attorney has no idea what you plan to do, but it will bother the counselor. It could even stop the lawyer from bumping more jurors from the panel.

After you leave the courtroom, send the attorney a letter of protest. Say that you think you would have been fair and impartial. A sample letter can be found following this chapter.

Should the lawyers spare you and allow you to serve, consider during your deliberation why those other people weren't good enough to serve. Be skeptical of an attorney's case that required rejection of your fellow jurors.

Solution 5
Make Your Representatives Listen

Our entire legal system is entrusted in the hands of judges, lawyers, and legislators. Citizens have some say in matters, but the input of the population at large has been diluted by crafty attorneys and talented judges. That group of legal scholars stole jury trials from America. It's time to reclaim the right to participate in juries.

Changes in jury selection probably won't come from lawyers because of severe conflicts of interest. The most obvious one is money. Anything that streamlines the legal system will sacrifice legal jobs. However, there is a more critical conflict.

Most attorneys represent several different clients at one time. With so many customers, they are likely to be representing numerous inconsistent positions. An attorney might represent a rapist and a rape victim on the same day. By supporting a change, regardless of the change, some clients could be harmed. Therefore, lawyers aren't zealously representing those clients unless they resist change. And oddly enough, by resisting change, many other clients miss the benefit of it. Because lawyers must represent individual clients at a micro level, most can't ethically work on the big picture to improve the system. Hence, it can reasonably be argued that most attorneys are ethically bound to maintain the system as it is today.

Judges can't do it either. Keeping the system inefficient assures their positions, but even more, they lack the power to efficiently change the system. Courts must sit passively and wait for a controversy to come into their courtroom to make a legal decision. That means it could take years, or even decades to change something through the courts. The Supreme Court started looking at violations of equal protection in jury selection over 100 years ago. They still haven't finished arguing it. We can't wait another century for the Court to do the right thing.

Only the legislature offers the possibility of a swift solution. While I don't mean to endorse all elected representatives as people who want to remedy problems, it is only through them that citizens can pursue a meaningful mission of self-help to fix the system. Letters, faxes, and phone calls can affect the judiciary and the legal community. However, as stated above, that group is relatively impotent to correct the flawed system. Those same messages can be tremendously effective when directed at the legislature.

When President Clinton nominated Zoe Baird for Attorney General of the United States, the media splashed her past. She had knowingly hired an illegal alien to take care of her children. Then she ignored paying social security on the employee.

While this might not seem to be a horrible offense for the average citizen, it greatly offended the population as a whole that the highest ranking law enforcement person in the country would have so callously violated the immigration law. How could Baird effectively enforce deportation positions with that monkey on her back? Phones rang overtime in Washington until the nominee withdrew. What citizens learned is that the people in Washington will listen if there's a focus. When public opinion is trained on a single issue, even senators listen.

We can solve the crisis in our courts. To go to your representatives with the bag full of problems pointed out in this book might cause you to be given lip-service and no action. Therefore, one issue must be singled out and resolved—jury selection.

Voir dire and peremptory challenges are playthings that lawyers use to manipulate justice. Law should be more than a game of pawns and gambits; it should be a quest for truth. Attorneys need to put away their toys and act mature. Since it's unlikely that lawyers will voluntarily stop abusing jurors, peremptory challenges and voir dire should be stripped from them.

We live in a time when everyone is looking to cut government waste. Few, if any, programs the government has ever developed are as wasteful of time, resources, and dignity, as voir dire and peremptory challenges.

To effect an end of voir dire and peremptory challenges, citizens must be heard. Their best recourse is to contact their local and federal legislators, because statutes can overcome the games of lawyers and judges. Legislators need to be sent a message that their constituents are highly offended that they're deemed competent to vote yet too bigoted to be jurors. Send the letter!

Solution 6
Abolish The Indian Defense

As a trial attorney, I've used voir dire and peremptory challenges to shape juries. In the past, I've represented several Native Americans on matters. When people speak of minority issues, they frequently mean African Americans. Blacks account for approximately 12 percent of the population, Indians, less than 1 percent of it. Native Americans are a tiny minority.

Being from that small of a group, one thing is assured. Indians never get a jury of their peers. When an Indian is on trial, the chance of seeing another in the jury box is remote. Should a lone member of a tribe be called, the opponent swiftly rejects the prospective juror with a peremptory challenge.

Since my Indian clients have no chance of ever getting a jury of their peers, I developed a special defense for them. I usually employ it only when the client has no "real defense." That is, he has no legally accepted excuse. The defense has so little to do with justice, I'm embarrassed by it. However, lawyers are always trying to stack the deck for their clients. Since voir dire and peremptory challenges allow me to mold a "fair and impartial" jury, I use the tools.

I start by asking jurors what my client's ethnic background is. It takes a while, but eventually a juror will volunteer that my client is an Indian.

Now I go to work on emotions by asking unending questions about whether they had unpleasant experiences with Native Americans. Jurors are asked if they moved away from an area because of them, if they think Indians have too many rights, drink too much, are too lazy, and dozens of other questions. I point out that jurors were hesitant to even acknowledge my client was a Native American. Then I force every juror to promise to disregard that my client is an Indian while making their decision on the case.

Throughout the trial, I remind them of the promise and close the case with pleas that go to the jurors' emotions, often without regard to the facts. The design is to make the jurors believe that if they find my client guilty, it's only because of their prejudice against Native Americans.

The defense works with any group that a client fits into. If I represent someone who is female, black, Italian, or a firefighter, the same defense occasionally wins. If voir dire were eliminated, this line of rubbish would be much tougher to get jurors to swallow. It only works if you set it up from the origin of the trial. The Lady of Justice is raped every time a defense like this graces the courtroom.

You can stop this misuse of the system. All you need do is send the letter to your representative stating your disdain for our current jury-selection process. Send the letter!

Solution 7
Fix The System

Sometimes fiction can show issues more clearly than any actual cases. The following is a brief summary of a portion of a new novel, *The Grey Avengers,* which graphically exposes several flaws in our system:

While out for a walk, an elderly couple were enjoying life when death came crashing upon them. A sports car driven by a spoiled brat raced down the street, veered off the road, and toppled Michelle Rosen, killing her.

The driver had been drinking heavily before taking his "toy" for a spin. Killing a pedestrian was nothing but a nuisance to the driver. He was certain that Daddy would fix everything. Which is exactly what Daddy did, by purchasing the best defense that $500,000 would buy.

Shaken by the tragic death of his wife, Irwin Rosen tried to adjust to the tragedy as he waited for the trial of his wife's killer. It was there that Rosen would be forced to relive the horror, not once, but repeatedly. First, the prosecutor would walk him through the testimony. Rosen was prepared, but he knew that tears could well up and his voice might crack as he struggled through an account of the death crash.

After completing his troubled story, he could be ravaged in a grueling cross-examination from sleazy P. K. Kaplan, a powerhouse attorney hired by the brat's Daddy. Kaplan was so concerned with justice that he said: "I'm not out to see justice done, I'm out to win a verdict for my client." All he cared about was money and winning. He argued that, "The practice of law is an art form, and winning cases is great art."

When confronted about seeking the truth, he advised a young lawyer that: "Truth doesn't win cases, lawyers win cases. Seek winning judgments, not absolute truth."

Kaplan's adversary was an experienced prosecutor who touted the highest conviction rate in a four-county area. Claymore Williams III ambitiously sought the proper case to "launch the next phase of his career." After a jury was selected to hear the case, the two champions met for final plea negotiations. Williams had a powerful case, except for a flawed blood sample that was taken from the defendant. It was that sample that was necessary to prove the driver was drunk. Williams had hidden the defect in the evidence from Kaplan, and hoped it would go undiscovered. Even if Kaplan caught it, Williams figured "he could outbluff the sonofabitch." He sought a manslaughter conviction, and nothing less would do.

During a jarring negotiation session, skillfully laid out by the author, the attorneys postured and fenced as Kaplan dropped hints that old ladies aren't too important and old men don't make good witnesses. Finally, the defense attorney fired his killer arrow. "There's a little matter about some blood..."

Claymore William's face went slack.

"… Did you honestly think you could keep that from me… that I wouldn't have bothered to check on who drew the sample? That I wouldn't find out the person was unqualified to gather the evidence? My God, man, getting clients off on technicalities is my speciality. Your case just got blown to hell."

After blowing the prosecutor's case apart, Kaplan offered: "Listen, when I said you had no case that was an exaggeration. Obviously, if I really believed that I wouldn't be offering to plea bargain in the first place. But your case is flawed. What the jury will do under such circumstances is anybody's guess; what you've got, basically, is a crap shoot. Now, honestly, I don't think you want to risk losing a case like this—particularly on a technicality. It's going to make you look bad. Maybe even sour your career."

A defeated Williams lost the edge as he pleaded with Kaplan to allow the state to save face: "Just a year in jail… he could be out in four months with good behavior."

"No jail time," Kaplan replied again, more firmly this time.

"How about community control… a few years of house arrest coupled with a rehab program and some community service?"

"No form of incarceration—in jail, at home, anywhere. That's non-negotiable."

Williams caved in after weighing what was best for the citizens of Hillsborough County and what was best for himself. A plea bargain posed the least risk to his career and, if he did try the case in court, he could lose. At least with the plea bargain Claymore could be sure the defendant was getting *some* form of punishment. He responded: "You realize your client is guilty as hell. If we just decided this case on the basis of common sense, he'd be behind bars in less than 24 hours."

"A reasonable assumption," P. B. concurred. "But if cases were decided on the basis of common sense we wouldn't need lawyers now, would we? You know and I know that a case isn't decided on common sense—even the weight of evidence—it's decided on the skill of the attorneys involved. We're not practicing in a court of law, we're practicing in a court of lawyers. Want proof?" Kaplan crowed proudly. "If lawyers didn't make a difference in courtroom verdicts why would I be paid so much more than my less illustrious counterparts?"

Then the prosecutor asked why Kaplan waited until the day of trial to bring forward the flaw of the case. The defense attorney responded: "The courtroom is a stage and we are the players. Waiting till the end to strike a plea bargain is far more dramatic and exciting than settling early, before one can build things to their proper climax. Besides," Kaplan noted, lowering his voice to a conspiratorial level, "… clients accept my fees with far fewer complaints when they see a jury selected and realize their case is actually coming to trial."

Rosen and a friend sat in the courtroom waiting for trial the next day when the two attorneys "did justice." They approached the bench and proffered the plea bargain. A reluctant judge listened before freeing the defendant in accordance to the lawyer's plea agreement.

After court, Rosen's friend screamed at the dejected widower, "A technicality! How could they let him go on a technicality!?" Then he asked Rosen what he knew about the plea bargain.

"I knew nothing about anything. I was supposed to be a witness." Rosen said it was hopeless, and nothing could be done about it. Then he said, "The wrong sonofabitch took the blood… there was no proof that Michelle was walking where I said she was… *that's* what the prosecutor said!"

Now, after considering the case as laid out, who do you blame for the travesty of justice? Who is the rottenest character in the story? My interpretation follows:

1. The defendant. If he hadn't driven drunk, none of this would have happened. Anything that slimy people do after the fact is dressing. The driver is the bad guy.

2. Next worst is the person who drew the blood improperly. It's because of incompetents like him (or her) that we have all these cases pleaded out because of technicalities.

3. The system is next on my list. We've developed a legal system of mazes where procedure controls over substance. We are in love with rules and ignore reason.

4. Next is the prosecutor, however, I don't know how mad to get at him. The author has painted him as such a stupid sonofabitch that he's just acting out his Machiavellian personality. His great conflict was wrestling whether this case would help or hurt his career. Then he negotiated away a case without talking to interested parties. I don't think the dumbest prosecutor I know would ever do that in a vehicular homicide case. He shouldn't have the power to do it. That problem goes back to number 3, the system. Prosecutors have too much discretion to charge or to dismiss cases. Further, it was the prosecutor who withheld the flaw in the evidence. No prosecutor with integrity would do that. At least in my state, we deal above the table. The more I think about the prosecutor, the higher I would place him on the blame list.

5. I give next honors to the defense attorney. While he is painted as a dog, he is doing his job the way the system has set it up. He has to defend his client to the fullest of his abilities. He's just a typical sleazy lawyer.

6. The judge comes next. He cleared the deal cut by the lawyers. He had the last clear chance to negate the lawyer's bargain.

7. Finally, I fault Daddy for raising the brat and bailing him out of trouble. This case only confirms what everyone knows: that money, power, and lawyers control the flawed system. People and justice just stand by and take it. It's time for change. Send the letter!

But what everything keeps coming back to is the system. The excerpts from this marvelous fiction hammer my message. Take *your* system back from the lawyers. (Published by Gollehon Press, *The Grey Avengers* was written by Marvin Karlins.)

Solution 8
Picking Our Jurists

Judges earn their seats by appointment or election. As discussed in the chapter dealing with judges, both methods of judicial selection have problems.

Federal judges are appointed for life and it requires an impeachment to remove them. Their terms should be limited.

It's been reported that President Clinton has inherited 115 judicial seats to fill, and he will probably appoint justices who are liberal. Reagan and Bush primarily spent their appointments on conservatives. What this causes is judicial battle. Judges on the bench often fight philosophical battles with one another, instead of doing justice.

A study of Supreme Court opinions shows how the law is always in flux. If the court is primarily composed of conservatives, death penalties abound, abortions are denied, and police rights are expanded. When the court has more liberals on it, the electric chair gets put on hold, abortions proliferate, and individual freedoms are given greater deference. Here's the problem: When you pick judges who are partial to the right wing or the left, they have usually made up their minds on critical issues, hence, they are prejudiced. Issues don't get fair consideration. If judicial appointments favored more moderates who lacked strong biases on issues like abortion and the death penalty, we would have more justice.

When considering elected judges, their terms should likewise be limited. We don't need permanent judges.

Further, attorneys and litigants should be banned from endorsing judges or contributing to judicial campaigns. There is such an appearance of impropriety in this that it can't be squared with reason. At least subconsciously the judges will lean toward those who supported them and away from those who opposed. That's in the best case, when a judge is trying to be fair. However, in many cases the favors will be tendered with deliberate partiality. No case should be decided because of a generous contribution, and none should even appear to have been.

Solution 9
End Courtroom Dilemmas Of Justice
Versus Player's Gain

When a party goes to court, his case is all that should be decided. Everyone connected with the matter should be concerned solely with doing justice. This basic principle is violated regularly, and should be stopped.

It's common for attorneys to write about cases they tried. Less frequently, judges and jurors do it. There is great danger in allowing this to continue.

The parties are supposed to receive an impartial trial. When players who can affect the decision have outside interests, justice can suffer. A juror on a case could subconsciously shape the size of the award or vote for the death penalty to make a saleable story for a book publisher or to sell their story to *A Current Affair*. Judges, lawyers, and litigants could do the same thing. It would be wise to ban participants in any trial from selling any information they receive in court.

Solution 10
Show Lawyers Their Conflicts Of Interest

Attorneys need help from citizens. They can't or won't see many conflicts of interest because when they refuse cases it hits their pocketbooks.

Lawyers are bound to zealously represent their clients. They are supposed to exercise independent judgment. Whenever an attorney represents two parties in any suit, there's a potential conflict of interest. Decisions which help one, often injure the other.

Imagine that the same advertising agency handled Pepsi *and* Coke. Every time they raised one client's market share, it would lower the other's. That's a classic conflict of interest.

The same thing happens in court cases. When a lawyer represents two plaintiffs, those two are in competition for a limited amount of defendants' dollars. Again, there is a classic conflict of interest.

The attorney can't use independent judgment when representing two clients in the same suit. Even the most innocent-appearing cases are fraught with potential conflicts. Therefore, lawyers should be barred from representing more than one party in a lawsuit unless they can clearly demonstrate no possible conflict of interest is present. If the one-party-one-lawyer rule is adopted, attorneys would police themselves quite effectively. Any time they handle more than one party, they'd be on line to be sued if either party they represented disliked the results.

Solution 11
Limit Court Access To Frequent Filers

Two groups of people grab too much court time for civil matters. They are the frequent filers of the legal system. One group contains petty plaintiffs, who sue everyone who crosses their path. The other is composed of weasels who won't honor obligations and must be sued to part with money they owe others.

Both abuse the system. Ordinary people can't get a case heard because these people have jammed the court dockets with their excesses.

Some people must love to go to court; it's almost an addiction to them. Maybe they're frustrated lawyers. Perhaps their court time should be rationed.

Instead of assigning court dates first-come-first-serve, they could be determined by the composition of the parties. Defendants who must be sued constantly should have their cases heard first. They shouldn't be allowed to use the courts for stalling.

Next priority would go to the cases of first-time plaintiffs. Frequent litigants could get standby treatment, with their cases heard after other litigants got their day in court.

Lawyers wouldn't be prone to represent frequent filers on contingency if they knew that their litigant could have his case bumped any time. Parties who have abused the system should be given the last seat on the back of the bus, and only then if there is room.

Solution 12
Watch For Infrequent Filers

The flip side of the frequent filers are the people who would never sue. One should always be alert for these citizens. They can be spotted by their repulsed looks cast upon someone who advocates the tort lottery. Infrequent filers strive to avoid conflict. When you locate one, take heed, for those are the people to do business with. In our litigious society, all others should be approached and dealt with cautiously.

An arguable example of a group of infrequent filers are devout Christians; they usually don't sue one another. This is because if they follow the teachings of Chapter 18 in Matthew, they must settle disputes amongst themselves. The process requires that the victim discuss a problem with the wrongdoer—privately—in hopes of reconstructing a relationship. If that fails, then a few witnesses listen to the parties discuss the situation and the party deemed to be at fault is asked to correct the wrong. Should this fail to resolve the issue, the church decides the matter, and if the church is ignored, the party at fault is banished.

When considering this specific method of dispute resolution laid out in the New Testament, one might question the

.cs of Pat Robertson. He is obviously a good Christian, yet his group of lawyers are reportedly pledged to sue into the next decade and beyond, fighting the likes of the ACLU and others who they think undermine Christian rights and values. This appears hypocritical. I wonder if it causes Robertson to lose any sleep?

Solution 13
Form Sue-ers Anonymous Groups

When people become obsessed with alcohol, drugs, or gambling, they often ruin their lives and anyone in their paths. Everyone knows that compulsive gamblers, alcoholics, and drug addicts need help with their problems. Support groups such as Alcoholics Anonymous and Gamblers Anonymous help these troubled people.

Sue-ers frequently have the same type of problems as alcoholics and gamblers. They will often risk everything on a court case, wagering their entire fortune on the toss of a judicial coin. Whether they win or lose, the same people might be out the next day looking for another lawsuit. Other litigants sue because they like the power or the thrill the process allows them. For some, litigation is a hopeless addiction; lawyers are their pushers.

People must realize that many litigants are troubled and unable to help themselves. Several steps can be taken to assist compulsive sue-ers. None of the following proposals are presented to punish the frequent filers, but are offered to assist them and to protect their victims.

First, if a defendant believes he is being pursued by a compulsive sue-er, he should be able to plead as a partial defense that the plaintiff is troubled with litigation sickness. The court will then consider the validity of the position, and have the power to order treatment for the plaintiff. Severe sanctions should be placed upon a defendant who is found to have frivolously claimed the plaintiff is a compulsive sue-er to discourage abuse of the defense.

Second, a defendant should be allowed to argue before the judge or the jury how many times the plaintiff has gone to court. Even if the plaintiff is not suffering from compulsive litigation sickness, his prior behavior should be relevant. It would certainly help the jury to know that a man was unlucky enough to walk in front of slow-moving buses on several occasions. It would show that the man is possibly unfortunate, probably careless, or in the worst case, deliberately looking for the tort lottery.

Third, we should not facilitate compulsive sue-ers. Any alcohol counselor will tell family members not to enable the alcoholic's disease. That is, don't give him an excuse to drink and don't accept excuses for why he drinks. We need to do the same with compulsive sue-ers. They need treatment, not an award or a settlement.

Unless we want to sever our country like Yugoslavia did with massive unrest and unending lawsuits, we must control our trips to court. Many litigants can't help themselves. We need to help them. We could start by opening a chapter of "Sue-ers Anonymous." In that type of setting, compulsive sue-ers would be free to discuss their perjured testimony, faked accidents, malingered claims, vindictive filings, bogus defenses, or other opportunistic lawsuit abuse.

In assessing the problem sue-ers, we must consider that either side could have the problem. Defendants can suffer from the same sickness.

Solution 14
Control Lawyer's Greed

Lawyers often take tort cases on a contingency. What that means is if the attorney wins money for the plaintiff, the lawyer takes a percent of the haul. The amounts can vary from 25 percent to 50 percent of the gross winnings.

Critics say that this demeans the profession of law and encourages litigation. While that may be true, it seems that attorneys should have the right to charge fees any way they choose. While I don't think it's a great system, I'm not sure that we should interfere with attorney's fee agreements. Further, some important cases are taken on contingency. Poor people might be without a chance of redress if contingency cases were eliminated.

Also, there's a group of lawyers who are unscrupulous and disreputable. These weasel attorneys will always find their share of slimy clients. Even if contingent cases were outlawed, the worms would burrow through the mud to find an alternative. At least with contingent fees openly accepted, those lawyers will be playing above board on *one* issue.

Jurors need to be aware of contingency fees, and be skeptical of impassioned arguments lawyers make concerning the value of a life or an injury. You see, attorneys are just salespeople trying to persuade jurors to buy their goods. Like a car salesman, they will try to charge the jury the highest price they can because their income is based upon how big an award the case produces.

However, consumers can only get gouged so much at car lots. The dealers set limits on how much a salesman can charge a customer for a given product. But lawyers have only their conscious to constrain them. They will often ask jurors for egregious sums, and sometimes, the jurors buy the whole line. Jurors need to protect lawyers from their own greed.

If we want less litigation, there must be an attitudinal shift. We should stop applying bandages over the problem.

No matter how well a lawyer presents the case, an inmate who intentionally shoots himself should pay his own medical bills, not win millions. Awards need to cover out-of-pocket costs if an accident strikes. Jurors can control lawyer greed by denying them huge verdicts and limiting awards to reasonable compensation for an injury. To receive more is unfair and to ask for more is deserving of scorn.

Solution 15
Close The Bedroom Door

An entire chapter was devoted to sexual misconduct cases. It focused on the inequities of the system. Victims who want privacy are paraded around, as if they haven't been humiliated enough by the assault. But the accused also goes through hell, whether guilty or not.

Since sexual abuse is so easy to charge, and nearly impossible to defend, can there be a solution? I think so. Consider that most sexual cases are unsubstantiated. Exceptions are egregious abuses like Tailhook, where crude behavior abounded with ample circumstantial and testimonial evidence supporting the charges. Gang rapes and other flagrant assaults also have many witnesses. Those matters don't apply to the following suggestions. The only cases I propose to solve at this time are the troublesome "he said—she said" ones.

First, publicity must be minimized. This goes against my grain as a strong First Amendment advocate, but the disastrous situation we have today is more troubling than the right of the free press to turn every citizen into a voyeur. We've got to switch off the CNN rape spectacles. The way to do this is simple. A procedure should be followed in all *civil* and *criminal* cases of sexual misconduct that assures discretion and secrecy is maintained until the defendant is proven to be a masher.

All sexual allegations, civil or criminal, should be first screened through a magistrate. He or she would review the reports and determine if there is probable cause to allow the case to go forward. This magistrate must be impartial toward men, women, prosecutors, and defendants.

Under this system, Mia Farrow, Anita Hill, Patricia Bowman, and Desiree Washington would have all taken the same course. However, after an investigation, the reports and statements would be turned over to a magistrate. Those reports should not have the names of the victims or the defendants in them. The magistrate could then decide them factually, not emotionally.

If the magistrate says there isn't enough to go forward, the case could be supplemented and resubmitted for consideration. There would be no limitation to the amount of times any case could be submitted.

Only after a hearing officer decides there's enough evidence to go forward with the case is the defendant apprised of the allegations. At that point he has an opportunity to rebut them. All statements and reports made by either party must be inadmissible in any upcoming trial. Nothing said or referred to at the preliminary hearing should be used against either party at the trial. What this avoids is accusers and accused being forced to hold back evidence to protect their chances at trial. Even total reversals of testimony from preliminary hearing to trial shouldn't be discussed before the jury. Lies should be dealt with in separate proceedings for perjury.

If the defendant fails to appear or is unable to rebut the allegations, then a trial date is set. The trial will be held in a *closed* courtroom, without spectators or media. Likewise, all pleadings and court files will be sealed from the public. If the defendant shakes off the charges, there will be no public reporting of the case. The defendant's reputation won't be blemished by unfounded allegations. If the plaintiff snares a victory, the results, but not the name of the accuser will be publicized. That way everyone would learn that Mike Tyson committed rape, but nobody would know that William Kennedy Smith was acquitted, or for that matter, even charged.

To assure that a party doesn't leak the matter to the press, severe sanctions would be imposed if *unsubstantiated* accusations become public. Accusers won't be trampled in public, nor will the accused. This solves the problem of victims of sexual abuse being put on trial. They won't have their names published. They won't be on television because their attacker was famous. Likewise, they won't be tempted by glory into making false charges.

Those accused won't have their names spoiled over rash allegations. They'll be able to defend in total secrecy, subject to publishment only if they're deemed to be mashers. Character assassination of both sides will be minimized, and whatever goes on is kept from outside voyeurs.

Some may say that only abuse will come of trials behind closed doors. To this I answer that we already have closed doors in most juvenile courts in the country. We also seal the court files on many sensitive matters. Also, our entire Constitution was written in total secrecy. Since matters couldn't be handled any worse than they are today with regard to sexual allegations, the secrecy would have to be a tolerated evil.

While it would be impossible to determine, my guess is that the largest percentage of innocent people serving time in jail is for the charge of rape by a stranger. Eyewitness identification is unreliable, especially when a person is being traumatized. I know of one case where a person was tried for multiple rapes. As the victims testified, each attempted to identify her assailant in the courtroom. One of the victims picked an attorney who was sitting in the courtroom's spectator seating.

Another victim picked a juror as the assailant. Despite these misses, the defendant was convicted on every charge. Perhaps the jury made the right call, but maybe not.

In addition to legitimate mistakes, there are less honorable reasons that cause innocent people to go to prison. A lying lady is difficult to beat in court. On the other hand, our current system is letting off a vast number of perverts who calmly lie, and lie, and lie.

When it comes to perjury, courts must grow fangs. Those teeth must flash regularly and rip into witnesses who give false testimony.

Solution 16
Learn Some Class From The Canadians

You might recall a huge flap when a female reporter was sexually harassed in the New England Patriot's locker room. The case was given an incredible amount of press and broadcast time. On the heels of that fiasco, Sam Wyche, coach of the Cincinnati Bengals, apparently wanted to avoid harassing of or by any female reporters. He flat-out barred them from the locker room. After refusing to let a woman reporter in the Bengal locker room, Wyche was heavily fined. He was asked if he regretted the incident and reportedly responded: "Hell no, I don't regret it. I'll never regret it. No amount of fine can make a man change his conviction... We didn't violate the spirit of the law. We married the right of equal access for all reporters to the right of human decency." Again, the press reported the matter so heavily that the sports pages across the country read like sexual tabloids.

A British magazine reported that the Canadian Football League faced a similar situation. The coach of the Winnipeg Blue Bombers of the Canadian Football League barred a woman reporter from their locker-room. He cited moral objections to her presence despite the CFL's equal-access rule for the press. It sounds almost like Wyche's rationale.

The commissioner of the Canadian league said, "In this case we really must look at the democratic process and I truly think that the process is defined as being the freedom of the right of action so long as it does not infringe on the rights of anyone else." The league believed that the coach was having his moral rights infringed. So, the parties were told to work out a mutually satisfactory arrangement.

The article ended with this sentence. "What causes a frenzy south of the border is handled in Canada with a calm that is typically Canadian." Can Americans learn anything from this? Apparently our northern neighbors can deal with sexual equality issues reasonably and quietly. They don't need to blast it on the front page of every newspaper for days. They don't need to scream "Wolf" at every corner. Dry British humor is panning our lunacy.

Americans are rugged, inventive, creative, and individualistic. But is everything that we've ever created a sacred cow? Is it possible that other nations have discovered a better way? Could sexual harassment issues be addressed more reasonably and effectively? The fabric of our flawed system is tattered. Nowhere is the cloth more ragged than in the field of sexual harassment. Unless a new suit is ordered, it needs a proper mending.

Solution 17
Use Alternatives To Litigation

The benefits of mediation and arbitration were described earlier. Both of these procedures are effective tools at clearing court calendars that are clogged by sue-ers.

It is logical to use both mediation and arbitration. When compared to court, they are informal and inexpensive. These alternatives offer equitable solutions. They are result oriented, with more concern about what happened and how to fix it than whether the parties precisely followed the proper judicial procedure.

Additionally, they can occasionally offer "win/win" solutions. In court, the decisions are frequently "win/lose" or "lose/lose." Where an alternative method of dispute resolution might repair injured relationships, courtroom battles generally embitter the combatants. People will be happier and more productive if they openly seek alternatives to litigation for settling disputes.

We must realize that many litigants avoid alternatives and race to court. Lawyers who barge into court without considering alternatives to litigation should be shunned.

Solution 18
Employ Class-Action Suits

Many times, a group of people are injured by a defendant. This can happen when an airline gouges its passengers or when a recording company pawns off a stage band as a celebrated star to enhance sales. Courts have devised a specific procedure to deal with cases involving multiple victims. It is called the class action.

Courts allow a few plaintiffs to present their cases in trial on behalf of the entire class. Several factors must be met before a class action is allowed. The class must be so large that it's impracticable to try all the cases. The claims and defenses must be typical for the few representing the class as the claims and defenses of the whole class. And the parties representing the class must adequately protect the interests of those who do not go to court.

Among the purposes for class actions are to avoid inconsistent verdicts and judicial inefficiency. Those seem to fit squarely into the message of this book, that is to make courts fairer and faster.

Like many solutions, they have a down side. Another message of this book has been to encourage people not to sue their neighbors. Class actions actually authorize attorneys to solicit potential litigants who fit into the class. Many people who sign onto the class would never consider suing if they had to be involved. However, with class actions, most people become invisible litigants. They don't have to go to court or ever participate. All they need do is apply to be in the class and wait for the court to decide if they have won a tort lottery. Class actions make it awfully easy for people to become litigants.

Another thing that class actions have going against them is lawyers generally take the lion's share of the award for the classes. With all said, class actions do streamline courts and equalize awards, so I support them as a viable alternative to multiple suits, but I would much prefer class arbitrations to class trials.

Solution 19
Establish Appeals On Facts

Scores of people have asked me how I can defend guilty clients. When I was a public defender, I had no choice. Any case dropped on my desk was mine. It was my job, and I had to defend everyone. That's why I developed the "Indian defense," because without it, many of my clients had none.

One thing that most people don't consider is that when lawyers plead for the life of a wretched killer, it's their duty to do so. The person will die if the lawyer fails. It's the same as when a surgeon cuts someone on the operating table. It doesn't matter to the doctor that he's saving the life of a notorious killer or the President of the United States. If the physician tries something drastic that works, he beats death. Lawyers do the same thing representing people who face the death penalty.

Lawyers get blamed for many things, but it's wrong to scorn them for representing bandits. If you were on trial, wouldn't you want your attorney to zealously fight for you?

However, the way many defenses are conducted is scornful. Lawyers representing clients who will likely be convicted—that is the evidence of guilt is overwhelming—perform strange rituals. They make the prosecutor jump through trap-laden procedural hoops and have the court make numerous rulings on admissibility of evidence. The reason is that for every ruling, there's a chance of an error being made.

Our appellate system, for the most part, cares little about the truth of the charge, but only that proper procedure was followed and the party received a "fair trial" under the "due process" clause of the Fifth Amendment. Since facts are basically incidental, lawyers set cunning traps to trick unwitting prosecutors and judges into committing procedural errors. When the defense lawyer succeeds in this game, the client is convicted, but the matter is reversed on appeal.

The defense attorney is advocating properly within the bounds of the law, that is, "the system." In fact, many would argue that it would be improper not to set all these snares. Because attorneys use (and abuse) the system, justice frequently suffers. It's common for mass murderers to have viable appellate issues while people wrongly convicted have none.

Something is terribly amiss when we worry more about whether the trial was "fair" than if the prisoner is "guilty." Often a convict believes he got a "bum" jury. The facts of the case point to innocence, but the verdict was guilty.

Once convicted, a person has two choices. Either accept the judgment, or appeal it. As indicated earlier, an appeal tests procedural fairness instead of weighing the proof of guilt.

I propose a new form of appeal for this type of defendant. Every criminal case could be video taped. If convicted, the defendant could review the video and decide if he wants a second jury to view the tape. If the convict chooses this method, procedural appeals should be waived. The second jury would decide if the conviction was proper by watching the tape, and their decision would be final—no further appeals would be allowed. If the second jury thinks the prior jury made a bad call, the defendant gets a new trial.

Solution 20
Unclog the Prisons

Our overcrowded prisons need some attention. We need to set priorities. If we want more jails, we must be prepared to pay for them. If we have enough prisons, then all that need be done is proper allocation of the cells.

There are many predatory criminals. They are the muggers, burglars, rapists, molesters, assailants, robbers, and the like. The most dangerous criminals should get the first beds in the jails. Should we have a surplus of prison space and determine that it's appropriate to put others in jail, then incarcerate the less dangerous people. It doesn't make any sense to release robbers to free jail space for anti-nuclear and anti-abortion protesters.

Solution 21
Establish A Value For Human Life

One way that people plan security is the purchase of life insurance. A young father might buy $100,000 on his life to protect his spouse from being destitute should she become a widow. In effect, the man is saying that his life is worth at least $100,000. The strange thing is that if he dies in the right type of accident, his wife can claim its worth a thousand times that amount.

Either we need to set a value on human life, or say its worth is impossible to determine. If a value can't be determined, then every case is a guess based upon how much passion overcomes the jury. Courts shouldn't be involved in guess-work and emotions.

Our courts have striven since the '60s to enforce civil rights. The main argument in civil rights' actions is that all people are equal. Our tort system is in direct opposition to civil rights; it discriminates wildly. One person's life is worth $105,000,000 in an auto fatality, while another is valued at a tiny fraction of that amount. It's unequal treatment under the law, and the courts should step up to do equity. Awards should be standardized if we really think all life is equal.

In Washington State, if an accident disables a worker on the job, the state pays between 60 percent and 75 percent of the lost wages. The amount paid depends on the worker's marital status and number of dependents. If a worker is killed, the survivor's spouse receives a similar percentage of wages for life, unless the spouse remarries.

Let the same worker die in an automobile accident unre-lated to work, and the spouse might receive nothing. Of course, the spouse might hit the tort lottery and take millions, while the spouse's wages would only have been thousands.

Also, if a worker lost a leg on the job, $54,000 would be paid. In the tort system, the award would run from zero to infinity. The civil tort system is fraught with unequal distribu-tion. As tough as it is going to be, we probably need to set a price on how much a human life is worth.

Solution 22
Eliminate Junk Science

Witnesses are generally barred from giving opinions in court. The reason is that it's believed that if the jury hears the facts, they can reach their own conclusions. An exception to testimony about opinions occurs when an "expert" tells what they think about an issue.

Courtroom testimony is flooded with opinions of experts. These are people who are so brilliant that they need to tell jurors how the world works, because jurors are too naïve to understand it themselves. Lawyers line up these hired guns to state their claims. For every expert with an opinion, another person in that field will contradict it. Attorneys then look for experts who can best sell their case to the jury.

Some cardiologists profess that heart attack victims should remain inactive to prevent further episodes. Others claim that exercise is the route to health and strength. While many doctors scream that smoking is harmful to health, the tobacco industry has no shortage of experts who testify that the links between smoking and illnesses are inconclusive. When experts get on the stand and give opinions, they're only saying exactly what the lawyer wants them to say, otherwise, the attorney would call another expert to testify.

Our system of justice would be well-served if experts were restricted to giving opinions only when it's overwhelmingly accepted that what they are saying is true. In the pure sciences, like physics, mathematics, and chemistry, experts can give opinions that are universally accepted by their colleagues. That's because the theories have been tested and proven.

However, when experts from the social sciences get involved, there is usually no way to test their theories. One economist says that government spending ends recessions, while another says private-sector development is the only way. One pediatrician recommends spanking and another recommends not to discipline children. Some teachers believe that "hooked on phonics" is the best way to learn how to read, while others think the sight-reading method is superior. A psychiatrist might certify a person to be mentally ill and another says he's sane. Some doctors claim that children never lie, while others say youngsters invent everything. None of these theories can accurately be tested.

Unproven opinions are confusing at best for juries. Junk science floods the courts as experts claim to know everything but can't agree on anything. One anthropologist actually claimed to be able to look at a footprint and tell who made the mark. She claimed that every person made individualized impressions, much like fingerprints. The problem was that these weren't impressions made by bare feet, but ones with shoes on. That's a little like trying to read fingerprints left by someone who was wearing gloves. Some prosecutors actually used this "doctor's" testimony to convict people. Juries believed the rubbish, yet I know of no other expert who supports this anthropological sleuth. How can our courts let this trash into evidence? We should return to Sergeant Friday's, "Just the facts, ma'am."

Even worse than wacky professional witnesses are the mercenary "experts." These people testify according to who pays them. Again, we have a situation where the wealthy and the powerful can parade the "best" evidence before the jury because they can afford the paid "experts." We can control "expert" abuse by severely restricting the use of opinion evidence in trials.

Solution 23
Blast Damages

In tort claims, out-of-pocket costs should be awarded to the wronged party. These would include repairs, lost wages or earnings, medical expenses, and other actual costs. The idea is to make the party whole, to pay them back for a wrong done them. The actual losses could be multiplied by a small factor to cover the inconvenience caused by the injury.

General damages, those not identified by dollar losses, like pain and anguish, should be awarded only when the behavior of the defendant is grossly negligent, reckless, or intentional. Unless the defendant grossly deviated from normal caution, general damages should be restricted.

Punitive damages should only be paid in certain cases of egregious conduct by the defendant. Since punitive damages are primarily to punish defendants, not to reward victims, the bulk of the punitive award could go to the state as a pseudo fine. Some states have begun tapping the exemplary damages, much to the chagrin of plaintiff's lawyers and their litigants.

Solution 24
Encourage Principle Suits

It's common for parties to claim, "It's not for the money, it's for the principle." When parties announce they are in it "for the principle," two things should happen to their case:

First, they should be transformed into "for principle" litigants and receive a free ride in our court. If they're out to better the world for whatever ideological reason, their filing fee should be waived. Also, if they succeed, their attorney fees should be paid by the losing party.

Second, they should be denied the right to get any money damages except their out-of-pocket costs—their special damages. General damages and especially punitive damages should be disallowed to a party suing or claiming to be suing for principle.

Solution 25
Control Emotions In Rendering Decisions

Many verdicts are based upon emotions rather than the facts. Jurors attempt to make the correct decisions, but we deny them the tools to put cases into perspective. They don't have anything to gauge their amount of award to tell if it's adequate or excessive. Sometimes the facts of the case inflame the passion of the jury and justice loses again.

We could solve this in several ways. Civil trials could be heard in two stages. First, the jury could decide if there was liability. If so, the judge could make the award based upon what like injuries under similar circumstances had paid. Then the jury never has to reach the dollar amount. Hopefully, judges would overlook passions and decide damages based upon injury alone.

If juries continue to decide the amount of damages, they could break them down on a scale rather than set a dollar amount. The jury could find for the party and declare compensation should be: none, minimal, adequate, ample, or extraordinary. The judge could then follow guidelines, like those used in workers' compensation claims, and rule on the actual amount of the award.

Solution 26
Establish Good-Faith Bonds

A bond could be required in civil cases to assure a plaintiff's good faith. The amount is unimportant. It could be as little as $500, and waived if the plaintiff can't afford it. If the defendant prevails, he wins the bond. Otherwise, the plaintiff is refunded at the conclusion of the suit. Even the requirement of a small investment will deter some of our frivolous suits from ever hitting the court.

Solution 27
Charge Plaintiffs For Additional Parties

It currently costs $120 to file a lawsuit in federal court. It doesn't matter how many defendants the complaint names. Lawyers, aided by the likes of consumer advocate Bruce Williams, aim to sue everyone in sight. Since it costs nothing to add a party, they greedily name anyone remotely connected to the case.

A stair-step approach to filing fees would make lawyers and their clients think about who they name in a suit. Perhaps, it could cost $120 for each defendant, or possibly $240 for the second, and $360 for the third. The rationale is that as more defendants appear in court, the complexity of the case increases, therefore the clerk of court can justify the added charges.

Solution 28
Limit Warning Labels

We should cease our quixotic pursuit of the ideal warning label. People must be presumed to have common sense. Anyone should know that if you climb a ladder, you can fall. Warnings should only be required for hidden dangers. Further, unless a product is excessively dangerous, warnings should be limited to a few words. If a dangerous condition is overlooked because too many warnings baffled the user, the over-warner should be liable for confusing the consumer.

Solution 29
Consider Anti-Deliberation

After a case has been presented to the jury, the panel is instructed in the law and they retreat to deliberate their verdict. The purpose is to have the committee reason out the proper decision. During this period, justice again gets a ride in the rumble seat.

Jurors are composed of both strong-willed and timid people. The leaders can sometimes sway the weaker ones into abandoning votes on grounds other than for equity. Everyone knows the quiet type; they're the people who would never raise their hand in school. Quiet people can get intimidated by braggarts.

There are few studies about deliberation of juries, but the most respected one revealed some odd conclusions. When jurors began deliberation, they often took a vote to see how everyone was thinking. In the first vote on criminal matters, the ballots might be seven for guilty, four to acquit, and one undecided, or any other mix that totals twelve.

The strange thing is that the majority position of the first vote controls the verdict in almost 90 percent of the cases. In those cases, whatever the majority thought on the first vote became the final verdict. When there are six votes for conviction, then the verdicts have a 50 percent chance of being innocent or guilty. This covers another 5 percent of the cases.

Five-percent of the cases ended with a stymied jury, unable to reach a decision, or hung. Ironically, the jury almost never hangs when the first ballot was split evenly. In those cases, deliberation appears to be of great value.

Since almost every case is decided by the first vote, the jury could just fill out a secret ballot after the trial, without discussing the case with each other. The majority would rule, and should there be an even split in the votes, then the jurors could deliberate, and attempt to come to a decision.

If the sample in the study is correct, fewer than 5 percent of the cases will split six-six on the first ballot. The weaker jurors will be heard on 95 percent of all cases, free from bullying in the deliberation room.

This means we could cease deliberation. By doing so, we would return to the concept of one person, one vote. We're after justice. Since deliberation does little but confirm the majority, then a secret ballot could decide the verdict.

Solution 30
Solve Complex Cases

Some people argue that cases can be so complex that jurors have no chance of understanding the issues. If a trial is too involved for a jury to grasp, then have a panel of judges or other experts decide the case. This would make sense in anti-trust, class-action, and other complicated cases.

Solution 31
Analyze Insurance Settlements

Insurance companies have an enormous advantage when dealing with claimants: They know the range of settlement for similar claims. Further, they are so much stronger financially than the claimant that they can stall and twist arms. To level the table a little, the following could occur:

When an insurance company and a claimant arrive at a settlement, a check for 10 percent of the settlement is tendered by the insurance company to the claimant. The proposal would then be sent to an independent screening organization which would rule whether it was reasonable or unreasonable. If the agreement is accepted by the committee, the insurer issues the remainder of the money to the claimant. Should the company find it to be unreasonably low, the claimant keeps the 10 percent check and starts negotiation anew.

One factor the panel should consider is the length of time it took to come to the agreement. Stall tactics used by the insurer should be discouraged. If the reviewing board believes the insurer delayed, they could reject the settlement as unreasonable because the insurer kept the money away from the claimant too long.

Solution 32
Give Little Guys A Chance

Since insurance companies have huge resources, they almost always have the upper hand in any settlement or suit. As discussed in the solution proposed above, insurers are regulated already, and a minor adjustment of those regulations would make the game fairer.

Another class of disputes poses the same inequities of economic disparity. When one of the parties has huge resources in comparison to the other, "Might makes right" and Goliath triumphs. Wealth invariably crushes the opponent, regardless of who is right. It happens regularly when someone has a dispute with their landlord, a department store, or an oil company.

Earlier in the book, I discussed how mediation and arbitration could be used to unclog the courts and give us more efficient justice. Litigation is complex, lengthy, costly, and frequently punishment-oriented. Mediation and arbitration can be swift, relatively fair, and serve as an "equalizer," especially when one party has vast resources.

When one litigant is an economic ant in comparison to the other, the little guy should have the option of forcing the case into binding arbitration. The parties would follow the decision of the arbitrator, and usually the arbitration could begin soon after the dispute erupted. The rich, therefore, couldn't stall proceedings until the little guy was squashed.

Solution 33
Burn Defensive Medicine

The estimated cost of defensive medicine is $25 billion a year. Medical expenses for treatment of all people injured in accidents are $30 billion. If we stop suing doctors unless there is gross deviation from reasonable practice, we could redirect $25 billion and provide free care to those injured in accidents at almost no additional cost to society. Under the current system, doctors, lawyers, insurance companies, and a few plaintiffs hit gold and everyone else pays for it.

Solution 34
Don't Test the English System

Under the English system, the loser pays the attorney fees for both sides. In America, the parties usually pay their own lawyers. The English way might restrict frivolous legal activity, but it could greatly affect the ability to get legal redress. The middle-class would have such a hammer over their heads that only the rich would dare venture into court. No one else could risk it. It doesn't make sense to try to bring equity into the system and then circumvent it by turning the courts into an exclusive country club.

Solution 35
Make Social Change Efficient

Lawyers fit an odd niche in society. While some of their work involves stabilizing matters, the bulk of it does nothing but make people miserable. Attorneys thrive on suffering. Much of their work is nonproductive for society. Their profession counters Adam Smith's theory that everyone's greed leads to the nation's betterment.

This isn't to say that lawsuits haven't corrected some problems. Litigation has made manufacturers sensitive to safety issues. Chain saws have emergency brakes, cars have seat belts, and children's clothes are fire retardant. But the cost of these benefits under the current system is too high. Lawsuits aren't an efficient way to improve society. And the costs of anticipated litigation gouges the public with needless "defensive" expenses. Many products and services are unavailable or prohibitively expensive because of the actual liability or the perception of legal exposure.

To reduce public misery, creative and talented attorneys should become productive instead of destructive. Those lawyers won't change without some impetus. They must be prodded into it or they'll continue on their path, dispensing grief and swallowing huge fees.

It's hoped that those advocates will channel their talent outside the litigation mill. Changing those legal counselors won't work unless most of the country transforms, too. Litigation should be the last resort, not the first card played.

Solution 36
Equalize Advocates

Another problem with our current flawed system of jury selection is more subtle. Everyone knows that good lawyers win more cases. The most authoritative study of juries revealed that it's a 20 percent advantage to have better counsel. Every time someone wins because of superior advocates, justice loses.

Noted attorney, F. Lee Bailey, wrote about it in his book, *The Defense Never Rests*:

When I entered law school, an attorney who later became a judge gave me a book and wrote on the flyleaf: 'Dear Lee, as you enter law school, bear this in mind. When I was a young man, not skilled, and overmatched by my opponents, I lost many cases that I should have won. But as I became older and more skilled and my opponents showing up were tyros, I won many cases that I should have lost. So in the end, justice was done.' His intent was lighthearted, but the inscription's truth is chilling.

To show how this can happen, a recent case involved two boys who jointly participated in rock throwing. A boulder was tossed off a freeway overpass and killed a motorist. Both juveniles pointed the finger at the other boy for throwing the killer rock. One boy got four times as much detention time as the other. The most apparent reason for the discrepancy was that one of the youths was represented by a high-profile attorney who clamps onto cases like a junk-yard dog. When I spoke to that lawyer about the case, he modestly rebuffed my proposal that his client received a better deal because of superior counsel, claiming that all he did was thoroughly investigate the case. I have to believe that the prosecutor didn't want to tangle with him.

Contrast this story with the blasting that Mike Tyson's attorneys received for their representation of the fighter in his rape trial. Some critics claim that poor lawyering is the reason Iron Mike went to jail.

The quality of the advocacy can affect an outcome. In an ideal world, all cases would be settled on matters of justice and equity, but we don't have that today. Better lawyers are also better jury pickers. If lawyers are forbidden to discriminate by challenging jurors, there will be more equity in the courtrooms. Juries will represent the people from the community instead of the attorney's "dream team."

Consider this frightening thought. A man who visited his son at David Koresh's compound claimed that "One day with Koresh, and I questioned everything in my life." He realized that he was almost taken in after a face-to-face meeting with the self-proclaimed Messiah. Imagine how persuasive a man like Koresh would be selling a bogus line to a jury. It happens every day.

For this problem, there is no solution.

Solution 37
Abolish Uneven Rewards

If a matter goes to court, the basis of compensation should be from real damages that are measurable. Why should some lives be worth zilch and others $105 million? Our system is haywire. Greedy plaintiffs bring in big dollars for lawyers and insurance companies. Everyone who wasn't involved pays the bill.

It's terrible when tragedy strikes, but money doesn't undo the injury. We need to stop using a system that gives millions to a few victims and spits on the rest.

We should stop being a nation full of wimps. People must accept responsibility for their actions and assume the risks of living. Walking or driving down a street is dangerous. Accidents happen, and people shouldn't have any incentive to be involved in one.

Today, they do.

Ben O. Fended
P.O. Box 0
Seattle, WA 98104
(206) 555-0879

Today's Date

The Honorable Slade Gorton
United States Senate
Washington, D.C. 20510

Dear Mr. Senator:

I am writing to express displeasure with our jury selection process. I find it offensive that lawyers are allowed to humiliate potential jurors by asking personal questions. While they claim to be seeking a "fair and impartial" jury, they are actually stacking the deck with panelists who favor their clients.

The entire process is insulting. The courts and lawyers actually presume that everyone called for jury duty is unqualified or incompetent to serve. After thoroughly demoralizing panelists with questions, the attorneys bump off jurors with peremptory challenges. The late Justice Thurgood Marshall condemned the practice as blatantly discriminatory. He recommended the abolishment of peremptory challenges if it is hoped for us to ever have juries that are representative of their communities.

Do you believe that anyone who is qualified to vote for you should be good enough to sit on a jury? If you do, please consider passing legislation to halt the harassment of jurors.

Sincerely,

Ben O. Fended

Ben O. Fended
P.O. Box 0
Seattle, WA 98104
(206) 555-0879

Today's Date

Charles Sleazly
Sleazly, Weazley, and Slyme
Attorneys at Law
321 Snake Street
Seattle, WA 98104

Dear Mr. Sleazly:

You probably don't remember me. I am the red-headed juror you unceremoniously dumped from the trial yesterday. The purpose of this letter is to inform you that I'm not the "ineddicated, vulgar, grovelling wretch" Dickens satirized in Oliver Twist. I would have been fair to your client, but you obviously were looking for someone who would be unfair to your opponent.

It humiliated me to be rejected as too bigoted to serve on your jury. I now understand the critics of peremptory challenges. You abused me, and I resent it.

Sincerely,

Ben O. Fended

Bibliography

Court Cases

U.S. Supreme Court cases:

Abbate v. U.S., 359 U.S. 187 (1959)

Apodaca v. Oregon, 406 U.S. 404 (1972)

Batson v. Kentucky, 476 U.S. 79 (1986)

Brown v. Mississippi, 297 U.S. 276 (1936)

Brown v. Board of Education, 347 U.S. 483 (1954)

Cassell v. Texas, 339 U.S. 282

Cipoilone v. Liggett, 60 L.W. 4703 (1992)

Daubert v. Merrell Dow Pharmaceuticals, Inc., 61 L.W. 4805 (1993)

Duncan v. Louisiana, 391 U.S. 145 (1968)

Florida v. Bostick, 59 L.W. 4708, (1991)

Garrity v. New Jersey, 385 U.S. 493 (1967)

Georgia v. McCollum, 60 L.W. 4574, (1992)

In re Gault, 387 U.S. 1 (1967)

Johnson v. Louisiana, 406 U.S. 356 (1972)

Miranda v. Arizona, 384 U.S. 436 (1966)

Neese v. Southern R.R. Co., 350 U.S. 77 (1955)

Pennzoil v. Texaco, 481 U.S. 1 (1987)

Sheppard v. Maxwell, 384 U.S. 333 (1966)

Spano v. New York, 360 U.S. 315 (1959)

Strauder v. West Virginia, 100 U.S. 303 (1880)

Swain v. Alabama, 380 U.S. 202 (1965)

Teague v. Lane, 489 U.S. 288 (1989)

United States v. Jackson, 390 U.S. 570 (1968)

U.S. v. Burr, 25 Fed. Cas. 15

U.S. v. Burr, 8 U.S. 469 (1808)

Selected statutes and official court reports – Federal and State

Periodicals

A Fair Jury, The essence of Justice, Irving Kaufman, *Judicature*, October 1967

Achieving Representative Juries: A System that Works, William Macauley and
Edward Heubel, *Judicature*, September 1981

Am Jur 2d Desk Book, 1992

Autoweek, Selected Articles 1991-93

Business Week, Selected Articles 1991

Consumer Reports, Selected Articles 1989-92

Economist, Selected Articles 1988-92

Esquire, Selected Articles 1989-90

Fortune, Selected Articles 1983-92

Friendly Exchange, Selected Articles 1988-92

Games People Play: The Devil Made Me Do It, Paul Luvera, Washington State Bar News, July, 1992

Harassment Charges: Who Wins?, Vincent Bozzi, *Psychology Today*, May 1989, p. 16

Harper's Magazine, Selected Articles 1990

Ideology and Criminal Rights, Time for Common Sense, Paul Savoy, *Current*, May, 1990

In the Valley of the Blind: A Primer on Jury Selection in a Criminal Case, Herald Fahringer, 43 Law and Contemporary Problems 116, 1980

Interrogations in New Haven: The Impact of Miranda, 76 Yale L.J. 1519 (1967)

Jet, Selected Articles 1985-93

Juror Selection and the Sixth Amendment Right to an Impartial Jury, John Ashby, 11 Creighton Law Review 1137, 1978

Juror Self-Disclosure in the Voir Dire: A Social Science Analysis, David Suggs and Bruce Sales, 56 Indiana Law Review 245, 1981

Jury Systems of the Eighties: Toward a Fairer Cross-Section and Increased Efficiency, Henry Dogin and David Tevelin, 11 Toledo Law Review 939, 1980

Mademoiselle, January, 1991

Miranda in Pittsburgh—A Statistical Study, 29 U. Pitt. L. Rev. 1 (1967)

Moody's handbook of Common Stocks, Selected Reports

National Review, Selected Articles 1989-92

New England Journal of Medicine, Selected Articles 1989-92

New York, Selected Articles 1991-92

Newsweek, Selected Articles 1989-93

Newhouse News Service, November, 1989

One Day/One Trial or a One Week Term of Jury Service: The Misleading Marketing of Modern Jury Management Systems, Michael Graham and Richard Pope, 45 Missouri Law Review 255, 1980

Parent's Right to Recover for Loss of Consortium in Connection with Injury to Child, Todd Smyth, 54 ALR 4th 112, 1987

Parade, Selected Articles 1982-92

People, Selected Articles 1989-92

Prevention, Selected Articles 1991-92

Presumed Innocent?, Richard Pollak, *The Nation*, November 11, 1991, p. 1

Procedural and Social Biases in the Jury Selection Process, Hayward Alker and Joseph Barnard, 3 Justice System Journal 220, 1977

Recovery of Damages for Loss of Consortium Resulting from Death of Child—Modern Status, John Wagner, 77 ALR 4th 411, 1990

Report of the Courts of Washington, 1990

Runner's World, Selected Articles 1989-93

Science News, Selected Articles 1989-91

Sports Illustrated, Selected Articles 1985-92

Standard & Poor's Register, 1992

The Constitutionality of Calling Jurors Exclusively from Voter Registration Lists, David Geronemus, 55 New York University Law Review 1266, 1980

The Constitutional Need for Discovery of Pre-Voir Dire Juror Studies, 49 Southern California Law Review 597, 1976

The Nature of the Beast, Anita Hill, *Ms.* January/February, 1992, p. 32

The Effect of Peremptory Challenges on Jury and Verdict: An Experiment in a Federal District Court, Hans Zeisel and Shari Diamond, 30 Stanford Law Review 491 (1978)

The Resignation of Vice President Agnew, New York Times, October 11, 1973

Time, Selected Articles 1988-92

Using Communication Cues to Evaluate Prospective Jurors During the Voir Dire, David Suggs and Bruce Sales, 20 Arizona Law Review 627, 1978

U.S. News and World Report, Selected Articles 1989-92

Vanity Fair, Selected Articles 1991-92

Vogue, October, 1991

Voir Dire: Establishing Minimum Standards to Facilitate the Exercise of Peremptory Challenges, Jay Spears, 27 Stanford Law Review 1493, 1975

Washington Monthly, December, 1990

Washington's Discretionary Immunity Doctrine and Negligent Early Release Decisions: Parole and Work Release, Marie Aglion, 65 Washington Law Review 619, 1970

Newspapers

Everett Herald, Selected Articles 1985-93

Grand Rapids Press, Selected Articles 1986-93

Los Angeles Times, Selected Articles 1989-93

New York Times, Selected Articles 1989-92

San Francisco Chronicle, Selected Articles 1988-92

Seattle Times, Selected Articles 1982-93

Seattle Post Intelligencer, Selected Articles 1982-93

Spokesman Review, Selected Articles 1989-92

USA Today, Selected Articles 1988-93

Wall Street Journal, Selected Articles 1988-93

Broadcast

ABC's 20/20, Selected Reports 1989-91

ABC's Nightline, Selected Reports 1990-92

CSPAN, Selected Reports 1992-93

Books

American Government, David Bender, Editor, Greenhaven Press, 1988

A More Perfect Union, The Making of the United States Constitution, William Peters, 1987

A Worthy Tradition, Freedom of Speech in America, Harry Kalven, Jr., Harper & Row NY, 1988

Aaron Burr, The Conspiracy and Years of Exile, 1805-1836, Milton Lomask, Farrar Straus Giroux, NY, 1979

American Jury, Kalven, Harry Jr. & Hans Zeisel, University of Chicago Press, 1966

Anatomy Of A Jury, The System On Trial, Seymour Wishman, Times Books, NY, 1986

Art of Questioning-Thirty Maxims of Cross-Examination, Peter Megargee Brown, Collier Books, NY, 1988

As You Like It, William Shakespeare, Octopus Group, London, England, 1985

Battle for Justice-How the Bork Nomination Shook America, Ethan Bronner, W. W. Norton, NY, 1989

Basic Ideas of Alexander Hamilton, Richard Morris, Pocket Library, NY, 1957

Before You Sue, Fletcher Knebel and Gerald S. Clay, William Morrow and Company, NY, 1987

Black Mondays—Worst Decisions of the Supreme Court, Joel D. Joseph, National Press, Bethesda, Maryland, 1987

Black's Law Dictionary, West Publishing, St. Paul, 1968

Bookbanning in America, William Noble, Paul S. Eriksson, 1990

Breach of Faith, The Fall of Richard Nixon, Theodore White, Reader's Digest Press, 1975

Civil War on Consumer Rights, Laurence E. Drivon, Conari Press, Berkeley, California, 1990

Cyclopedia of Practical Quotations, J. K. Hoyt, Funk & Wagnalls Company, NY, 1896

Conflict of Rights, Melvin Urofsky, Charles Scribner's Sons, 1991

Confronting the Constitution, AEI Press, Washington, D.C., Allan Bloom, 1990

Constitution of the United States, David Currie, University of Chicago Press, 1988

Courts on Trial, Jarome Frank, Princeton University Press, 1949

*Courage of Their Convictions*Peter IronsThe Free Press1988

Conspiracy Trial, Judy Clavir and John Spitzer, Bobbs-Merrill Co., 1970

Contracts, John Calamari and Joseph Perillo, West, St. Paul, 1970

Courage of Their Convictions, 16 Americans Who Fought their way to the Supreme Court, Peter Irons, The Free Press, a division of Macmillan Publishers, 1988

Criminal Law and Its Processes, Sanford Kadish and Monrad Paulsen, Little, Brown, Boston, 1975

Cyberpunk, Outlaws and Hackers on the Computer Frontier Katie Hafner & John Markoff, Simon & Schuster, NY, 1991

Decision in Philadelphia, Christopher Collier & James Lincoln Collier, Random House Reader's Digest Press, NY, 1986

Defense Never Rests, F. Lee Bailey.

Democratic Eloquence, Kenneth Cmiel, William Morrow, 1990

Doing Justice, A Trial Judge at Bork, Judge Robert Satter, American Lawyer Books, NY, 1990

Dolley Madison, Her Life and Times, Elswyth Thane, Macmillan Co., NY, 1970

Encyclopedia Americana, 1958 edition

Everybody's Guide to the Law, Melvin Belli and Allen P. Wilkinson, Harcourt Brace Jovanovich 1986

Fact About the Presidents, Joseph Kane, Pocket Books, NY, 1964

Federalist Papers, Alexander Hamilton, James Madison, John Jay, Heritage Press, 1945

Founding, A Dramatic Account of the Writing of the Constitution, Fred Barbash, Linden Press, NY, 1987

Franklin, David Freeman Hawke, Harper & Row, 1976.

Freedom at Midnight, Larry Collins & Dominique LaPierre, Simon & Schuster, NY, 1975

Genius of the People, Charles L. Mee, Jr., Harper & Row, NY, 1987

Great Courtroom Battles, Richard Rubenstein, Playboy Press Book, 1973

Growth Of The American Republic, Samuel Eliot Morison and Henry Steele Commager, Oxford University Press, NY, 1942

Grand Jury, the Use and Abuse of Political Power, Leroy D. Clark, Quadrangle, New York Times Books, NY, 1975

Handbook on Criminal Law, Wayne LaFave and Austin Scott, West Publishing, 1972

Handbook on the Law of Torts, William Prosser, West Publishing, 1971

Henry VI, Part Two, William Shakespeare, Octopus Group, London, England, 1985

Helmsleys, The Rise and Fall of Harry & Leona Richard Hammer, NAL Books, 1990

Hit Me—I Need the Money!, Marjorie Berte, ICS Press, San Francisco, 1991

Hitler's Justice, The Courts of the Third Reich, Ingo Müller, Harvard University Press, Cambridge, Massachusetts, 1991

Holy Bible

How Can You Defend Those People?, James S. Kunen, Random House, NY, 1983

How Free Are We? What the Constitution Says We Can Do, John Sexton and Nat Brandt, M. Evans & Co., NY, 1986

How to Avoid Lawyers, Edward Siegel, Fawcett Crest, NY, 1989

In Our Defense, The Bill of Rights in Action, Ellen Alderman and Caroline Kennedy, William Morrow and Company, NY, 1991

In Pursuit of Reason, The Life of Thomas Jefferson, Noble E. Cunningham, Jr.Ballantine Books, NY, 1987

Insanity Defense and the Trial of John Hinckley, Jr., Lincoln Caplan, David R. Godine, Boston, 1984

Jefferson and Monticello, The Biography of a Builder, Jack McLaughlin, Henry Holt and Co., NY, 1988

Joy of Cooking, Irma and Marion Rombauer, Bobbs-Merrill, NY, 1974

Judging the Jury, Valerie P. Hans and Neil Vidmar, Plenum Press, NY, 1986

Juries On Trial, Faces of American Justice, Paula DiPerna, Dembner Books, NY, 1984

Jury in America, John Guinther, Facts On File Publications, NY, 1988

Landmark Decisions of U.S. Supreme Court, M. Harrison and S. Gilbert, Editors, Excellent Books, Beverly Hills, California, 1991

Law of the American Constitution, Its Origin and Development, Charles K. Burdick, G. P. Putnam's Sons, 1922

Lawyers' Medical Cyclopedia of Personal Injuries, Allen Smith Co., 1981

Liability—The Legal Revolution and Its Consequences, Peter W. Huber, Basic Books, Inc. Publishers, NY, 1988

Looney Laws, Robert Wayne Pelton, Walker & Co., NY, 1990

Long Walk at San Francisco State, Kay Boyle, Grove Press, NY, 1967

Lure of the Law, Richard Moll, Viking, 1990

Make No Law—The Sullivan Case & the 1st Amendment, Anthony Lewis, Random House, NY, 1991

Man from Monticello, An Intimate Life of Thomas Jefferson, Thomas Fleming, William Morrow & Co., NY, 1969

McCormick's Handbook of the Law of Evidence, 2nd Edition, Edward Cleary, West Publishing, St. Paul, 1972

Mediate, Don't Litigate, Peter Lovenheim, McGraw-Hill Publishing, NY, 1989

Mourning Bride, William Congreve (1697)

Nature and Functions of Law, Harold Berman and William Greiner, Foundation Press, NY, 1972

Neighbor vs. Neighbor, Legal Rights of Neighbors in Dispute, Mark Warda, Sphinx Publishing, Clearwater, Florida, 1991

New Dictionary of Thoughts, Tryon Edwards, Standard Book Co., 1959

Of Law and Men, Papers & Addresses of Felix Frankfurter, Philip Elman, Harcourt, Brace & Co., NY, 1956

Oil & Honor, The Texaco-Pennzoil Wars, Thomas Petzinger, Jr., G.P. Putnam's Sons, NY, 1987

Oliver Twist, Charles Dickens, Oxford University Press, 1983

Orwell, Michael Shelden, Harper Collins, NY, 1991

Origins of the American Constitution, a Documentary History, Michael Kammen, Penguin Books, NY, 1986

Pay Dirt, James A. Albert, Branden Publishing Co., Boston, 1989

Population Explosion, Paul and Anne Ehrlich, Simon & Schuster, NY, 1990

Price of a Life, One Woman's Death from Toxic Shock, Tom Riley, Adler & Adler, NY, 1986

Quarrels that have Shaped the Constitution, John Garraty, Harper and Row, NY, 1987

Reader's Digest Almanac 1982 Almanac and Yearbook, Reader's Digest, NY, 1982

Reconsecrating America, George Goldberg, William B. Eerdmans Publishing Co., Grand Rapids, Michigan, 1984

Restatement of Torts, 2nd

Rights Talk, The Impoverishment Of Political Discourse, Mary Ann Glendon, The Free Press, NY, 1991

Signers of the Constitution of the United States, Brother C. Edward Quinn FSC, Bronx County Historical Society, 1987

Supreme Court of the United States, Its Beginnings & Its Justices 1790-1991, Commission on the Bicentennial of the United States Constitution, 1992

Street-fighter in the Courtroom, The People's Advocate, Charles Garry, E. P. Dutton, NY, 1977

Taking Liberties, A Decade of Hard Cases, Alan M. Dershowitz, Contemporary Books, NY, 1988

Texaco and the $10 Billion Jury, James Shannon, Prentice Hall, NJ, 1988

Theory of Freedom, Stanley I. Benn, Cambridge University Press, 1988

Thinking Under Fire, Daniel Kornstein, Dodd, Mead, & Co., NY, 1987

Thomas Jefferson & the New Nation, Merrill D. Peterson, Oxford University Press, NY, 1970

Thomas Jefferson, An Intimate History, Fawn M. Brodie, W. W. Norton & Co., NY, 1974

Trial by Jury, Steven Brill, American Lawyer Books/Touchstone, NY, 1989

Unequal Protection, Women, Children, and the Elderly in Court, Lois G. Forer, W. W. Norton, NY, 1991

Understanding American Government, Harris, Roberts, and Elliston, Little, Brown, NY, 1988

Verdict, The Jury System, Morris Bloomstein, 1968

War on Drugs—Opposing Viewpoints, Neal Bernards, Greenhaven Press, Inc., San Diego, California, 1990

We Hold These Truths, Understanding the Ideas and Ideals of the Constitution, Mortimer Adler, Macmillan Publishing, NY, 1987

Who Was Jack Ruby, Seth Kantor, Everest House, 1978

Wolf by the Ears, Thomas Jefferson and Slavery, John Chester Miller, The Free Press, NY, 1977

World Almanac and Book of Facts 1992, World Almanac, NY, 1992

World Almanac and Book of Facts 1993, World Almanac, NY, 1993

You and the Law, Jules Archer, Harcourt Brace, NY, 1978